YEADON'S REGISTER

of

L N E R

LOCOMOTIVES

Volume Forty-Six Part A

Classes J52, J53, J54, J55, J56, J57 & GNR J19

The Stirling Great Northern 0-6-0 Tank Engines

ISBN 1 899624 91 0

YEADON'S REGISTER OF L.N.E.R. LOCOMOTIVES - VOLUME 46A

EDITORS NOTE AND ACKNOWLEDGEMENTS

The Great Northern 0-6-0 tank engine fleet consisted basically two different types, the saddle tank and the side tank. The former type, introduced by Stirling and rebuilt by Ivatt and Gresley, is featured in this Part of Volume 46. Once again we present a host of information and photographs, compiled by Willie Yeadon over many years, and only now seeing the light of day. Part B will cover the side tank 0-6-0 introduced by Gresley and, in order to get them into a related volume, the locomotive fleet of the East & West Yorkshire Union Railway will also be included along with the 0-6-0T classes of the Midland & Great Northern Railway.

Yeadon's Register of LNER Locomotives has proved to be of enormous benefit not only to the railway enthusiast but also to the historian and especially the railway modeller. If you want to build a model of an LNER locomotive and have it painted to a specific period in time with all the correct fittings, then the *Register* will give you all the help you require.

This volume has taken the usual course of previous numbers and once again we must thank Eric Fry for his long association with production besides his commitment to ironing out any mistakes - thanks Eric. Mike, Roy and Tina, and the Amadeus Press are to be thanked for using their skills to bring this volume to press.

Next year the Yeadon Archive will be moving to a new, purpose built and more centralised premises, along with the rest of the University Archive, the Hull City Archives and Hull Local Studies Library. Therefore we could have a slight interruption in the production of one of the few remaining volumes of this series but if there is it will only be very temporary because the ladies would run the University Archive have everything ready and in hand for a, hopefully, painless transition. In the meantime we must once again thank them for their unstinting and much valued support.

For their continued support we thank Jean and Simon who continue to give their blessing to the project. Thanks.

With any series of this kind it could not carry on without its readers so, thanks to all of you also.

The catalogue references for the locomotives featured in this volume are as follows:
DYE 1/47; DYE 1/48; DYE 1/52; DYE 1/61; DYE 2/6; DYE 2/7.

We would also like to acknowledge the contribution from the following photographers, most of whom, sadly, are no longer with us: I.C.Allen, J.W.Armstrong, R.J.Buckley, W.A.Camwell, H.C.Casserley, G.Coltas, R.C.Copeman, A.B.Crompton, A.W.Croughton, D.A.Dant, C.E.Dixon, A.G.Ellis, N.Fields, A.G.Forsyth, E.V.Fry, P.H.Groom, L.Hanson, T.G.Hepburn, B.H.Hilton, P.J.Hughes, W.M.J.Jackson, J.M.Jarvis, H.N.James, C.Lawson-Kerr, R.A.Panting, H.Percy, L.W.Perkins, L.R.Peters, P.Ransome-Wallis, S.J.Rhodes, J.Robertson, J.F.Robinson, C.L.Romane, C.J.B.Sanderson, E.E.Smith, Neville Stead, Rail Archive Stephenson, W.H.Tate, D.L.Wilkinson, P.Wilson, W.H.Whitworth, W.B.Yeadon.

Volume 47 of Yeadon's Register will present the North Eastern 0-6-0 tender engines.

The Yeadon Collection is available for inspection and anyone who wishes to inspect it should contact:-

The Archivist
Brynmor Jones Library
University of Hull
Hull
HU6 7RX
Tel: 01482-465265

A catalogue of the Yeadon collection is available.

First published in the United Kingdom by
BOOK LAW PUBLICATIONS 2008 in association with CHALLENGER
382 Carlton Hill, Nottingham, NG4 1JA.
Printed and bound by The Amadeus Press, Cleckheaton, West Yorkshire.

INTRODUCTION

General

The story of the Great Northern Railway shunting engines is largely that of the saddle tank. Stirling introduced his standard type in 1874 based closely on his 0-6-0 tender engines. When Ivatt arrived on the GNR in 1896 he continued to multiply them with only minor changes in design, until the last ones were built in 1908. In all, Stirling and Ivatt produced 250 of these characteristic engines which were employed all over the GN system on shunting duties and short distance goods workings. The final development (LNER Class J52) lasted well into BR days, to 1961.

Gresley preferred a side tank design and his first engines of this type appeared in 1913. With modification it became, after Grouping, a Group Standard type and eventually totalled 102 engines, the last of which survived until 1965.

The strict economies practised by the boiler department during Ivatt's regime, which continued under Gresley, had a considerable influence on events. New construction of boilers was kept to the absolute minimum. Any boiler from a withdrawn or rebuilt engine thought to be capable of further use was set aside and examined for possible utilisation elsewhere on some other class of engine, particularly on Stirling's types. The boiler shop even resorted to lengthening or shortening the barrel, or in some cases shortening the firebox, in order to provide replacements. As a result there were many instances of engines receiving boilers not standard with the normal for that class, and the GNR 0-6-0Ts exemplified this.

This policy of economy persisted, and indeed grew, under Gresley to the extent that the first fifty of his own 0-6-0T design were built new with boilers that had been previously used. The first thirty (LNER Class J51) used 4ft 2in. diameter boilers displaced from Ivatt's 0-8-2T engines, suitably shortened, whilst the next twenty were given second hand 4ft 5in. diameter boilers of which many were standing spare at the time. Some of these engines never at any time carried a brand new replacement boiler.

In passing, it should be said that the same policy of economy applied to tenders (explained more fully in the Appendix volume covering GNR tenders). Many new engines were built and coupled to second hand tenders taken from older engines which in their turn took tenders from even older ones, the lower end of the scale receiving ancient but still serviceable tenders from scrapped engines.

Class J52 (GNR J13) and J53 (GNR J14)

Stirling's final saddle tank design (Class J14) appeared at the end of 1892, twelve months after the last J15 (LNER Class J54) had been built. It was primarily intended for use on the increasing exchange traffic via the Metropolitan Widened Lines to South London, although later multiplied for general duties throughout the system. Something stronger was required for this exchange coal traffic because of the steepness of Ludgate Hill bank from Farringdon to the bridge over the Thames. Weight considerations applied which restricted any great increase in either size or weight of the new design.

The first thirty engines of the J14 class were built at Doncaster in three separate batches of ten each: Nos.921 to 930 from December 1892 to June 1893, Nos.961 to 970 from July 1893 to March 1894, and then Nos.971 to 980 from August 1894 to October 1895. In 1896 another fifteen engines were supplied by Neilson & Co., Nos.1046 to 1060, all delivered during July. Five more, Nos.1211 to 1215, were built by the same contractor in June 1897, which were followed two months later by the final pair built by Doncaster, Nos.111 and 155. The total of Stirling's J14 had now reached fifty-two with the last twenty-two being put into traffic after his death in November 1895.

The overall length of the engines was the same as the engines in the final series of J15 (LNER J54), but the boiler was modified by increasing the length of the barrel by 5 inches. This rendered the boiler type no longer able to be interchanged with any other class. Because the firebox was repositioned in the frames, it was necessary to set back the coupled wheelbase by 5 inches. A larger saddle tank was fitted but the bunker was shortened by 7 inches.

The cylinders of the first few engines had a diameter of $17^{1}/_{2}$ins., the same as Class J15, but 18ins. was quickly adopted as the new standard.

When further saddle tanks were required, Ivatt continued to build to this design except that the boilers were now enlarged from 4ft $0^{1}/_{2}$in. to 4ft 5in. diameter and incorporated a dome. Eighty-five more engines were built from 1897 to 1909 and these were separately classified J13 (LNER J52). The new class was wider over the running plate, cab and bunker.

Ivatt made no attempt to rebuild the Stirling engines with domed boilers and indeed new boilers of the original type continued to be ordered as replacements as late as 1909. It was 1922 when Gresley commenced the rebuilding of Class J14 to J13, Nos.970, 977 and 1060 being done that year. The process came to an end in November 1932 when No.3979 was rebuilt. This left No.3928 still as Class J53. However, this engine was one of five fitted earlier with an intermediate size of boiler, with dome. No.3928 was an early withdrawal, in November 1935 but remained in Service Stock at Doncaster works until June 1936 when Class J53 became extinct.

The rebuilds got new wider tanks but retained their narrower cabs so that the higher pitch of the bigger boilers entailed replacing the circular font windows by oval shaped ones, a point of visual distinction.

Only one batch of spare boilers for Class J13 was ordered during GNR days, in 1904. The next lot of twenty were actually constructed at Stratford works in 1926-27 and sent to Doncaster for fitting. In the meantime between 1921 and 1927 fifty-two of Ivatt's standard 4ft 5in. diameter boilers were converted at Doncaster for use on Class J52 by increasing the length of the barrel from 10ft 1in. to 10ft 6in. There was an abundant supply of these second hand boilers at that time as a result of withdrawal of older engines and the steady rebuilding of more modern engines with 4ft 8in. diameter boilers.

Apart from the systematic rebuilding with 4ft 5in. diameter domed boilers, five J53 (Nos.3927, 3928, 3966, 4046 and 4211) were fitted with 4ft $2^{1}/_{2}$in. *domed* boilers during 1925-28, thus introducing a non standard version of that class. The four boilers concerned (one was used on two different engines) were obtained from withdrawn 0-4-4Ts of classes G1 and G2 - one boiler was already twenty years old. The length of the barrels had to be increased by five inches before fitting to the saddle tanks and of course alteration was required to the tanks for the dome. Despite these changes the engines concerned were not reclassified, even though they were barely distinguishable from Class J52.

Four of these conversions eventually received 4ft 5in. boilers, thus becoming J52. One of the four converted boilers was used again to reboiler No.3928, the others were scrapped. No.3928 remained a hybrid and was withdrawn in November 1935, the first withdrawal and the only engines not rebuilt to Class J52.

Four more engines were withdrawn before war broke out in 1939, when withdrawals ceased. One hundred and thirty-two J52 entered BR stock in 1948 and scrapping began again in 1950. The class became extinct in 1961, except for old No.1247 which has been preserved.

Boiler	*Ex*		*Onto*
1535	G2	765 Aug. 1924	J53 4211 Sept. 1925 — Apr. 1932
6908	G2	682 Aug. 1924	J53 4046 Apr. 1925 — Sept. 1930
7128	G2	3696 Apr. 1926	J53 3927 Oct. 1926 — Aug. 1929
7131	G1	940 Aug. 1924	J53 3966 May 1925 — Nov. 1927
7131	J53	3966 Nov. 1927	J53 3928 Sept. 1928 — Nov. 1935*

* To Service Stock. Cut up June 1936.

As shunting engines, the class was to be found wherever goods yards abounded and found more than half a century they took care of the shunting requirements of the GN, LNER and BR at these locations. Besides being found in the usual areas the length and breadth of the GNR system (the London area had over fifty of them at Grouping), a handful were to be found in the GN outpost at Manchester where their numbers rose after the LNER took over but by 1930 they had all returned to the east side of the Pennines.

They remained a fixture of the London area throughout the LNER era and into BR days. Pre-war the number allocated between Hornsey and King's cross sheds had risen to nearly seventy, virtually half the class. Mention has already been made of their exploits onto Southern metals via the Metropolitan but besides these trips the class took on other trip working onto the ex Great Eastern lines in and around the Capital. Outside of London New England always maintained a fair sized allocation of them as did Doncaster with numbers always in the upper twenties. In the West Riding both Ardsley and Bradford had a reasonable number pre-Grouping but as new J50 0-6-0T emerged from the makers in early LNER days their presence at these places was cut dramatically. Colwick maintained an allocation numbered in the teens throughout the history of the class but the final few worked from Ardsley shed until March 1961. In Departmental service Doncaster works kept a small number of the class until the last two were condemned a month prior to the Ardsley based pair. When No.68846 was withdrawn in May 1959 it was purchased privately for preservation and restored in GNR livery as No.1247 so that the J52 class lives on.

Class J54 (GNR J15) and J55 Rebuilds (GNR J16)

Class J15 were Stirling's first saddle tank engines with 4ft 8in. diameter wheels. Six were built in 1874 and by 1892 there were ninety-five in service. Except for ten built by R.Stephenson & Co. in 1891 - Nos.901 to 910, and ten supplied by Neilson & Co., also in 1891 - Nos.911 to 920, the rest were built at Doncaster at the approximate rate of a handful (2 to 9) each year from 1874 to 1892 excepting 1876, 1877 and 1884. Because of the time period from first to last engine built, numbering was somewhat random and ranged between 139 and 860.

Their boilers were domeless and measured 4ft 0½in. in diameter, these and the cylinders and the wheel spacing being the same as the contemporary 0-6-0 goods engines (GNR Class J6). The cabs had open backs except for the final twenty-seven engines (Nos.854 to 860 and the contractor built engines) which were enclosed.

The overall length had been progressively increased during the years of construction, giving four distinct series. The first six engines (the 494 series) were 29ft 6in. over buffers. The next ten (500 series) measured 30ft 6in. in order to accommodate stronger drawgear and a longer bunker. With the fifty-two engines of the 634 series (built 1880 to 1891) the bunker was further lengthened and the length over buffers became 31ft 1½in. Finally, with the twenty-seven engines of the 854 series, enclosed cabs (which were made wider) were provided and the bunker was yet again lengthened so that the over buffers measurement was now 31ft 9½in.

No changes were made to these figures down the years, even when larger diameter boilers were fitted, and none of the engines with open back cabs ever received the enclosed type. The LNER classified all those with open cabs J54/1, whilst J54/2 was given to the 854 series which had enclosed cabs.

Withdrawals and rebuilding to Class J16 resulted in fifty-six Class J54 becoming LNER property. Rebuilding and withdrawal continued and Class J54 became extinct in 1933.

In 1897 Ivatt reconstructed two Class J17 Nos.606 and 610 (J17 was a class of ten engines, a shortened version of Class J15 - *see* LNER J56). They were given Ivatt's standard 4ft 5in. diameter domed boiler, new tanks and an enclosed cab replaced the open back type. New frames were provided in order to accommodate the larger boiler, the wheelbase being increased to the same as the J15 class 500 series. Under the 1900 classification system these two engines took J16 and they formed the nucleus for the later rebuilds from Class J15. No more of the J17 class were thus rebuilt, the expense of doing so not being justified.

Nine years elapsed before any more engines were rebuilt to Class J16. Nos.606 and 610 were reboilered (again with the standard type) in 1904 and 1906 respectively and their discarded boilers were put to further use in the rebuilding of Nos.913 and 918 in 1906 and 1907 respectively. These two J15 were from the later 854 series so already had enclosed cabs. However, the larger diameter boiler required new tanks to be made.

In 1908 No.638 was also rebuilt, the boiler coming from an old single wheeler, No.61, which Ivatt had rebuilt with a standard domed boiler in 1898. No.638 kept its open back cab and the circular front windows were replaced by oval shaped ones to clear the higher pitched tank.

A period of indecision appears to have overtaken the GNR Locomotive Department. Not only were no further rebuilds made to Class J16 under Ivatt but three J15 were condemned in 1910 whilst ten new straightback boilers were ordered in 1911 and fitted as replacements during 1912-1915.

It was left to Ivatt's successor, Gresley, to rebuild the Stirling engines in earnest. Firstly, when he took over in 1911 he stopped further production of domeless boilers for Class J15. Secondly, Gresley decided that in future the standard general purpose boiler was to be 4ft 8in. in diameter instead of 4ft 5in. for fitting to the 4-4-0 (LNER D4) and 0-6-0 (LNER J4) classes, and others. This decision released a large number of 4ft 5in. boilers which could be put to further use on the saddle tanks. In fact so many became available that, except for

Eighty-five Class J52 engines, Nos.1201 to 1210, 1216 to to 1290, were built between August 1897 and February 1909. Nos.1216 to 1250 were built by contractors, the others were all manufactured at Doncaster.

In 1892 Stirling introduced his final saddle tank design, classified J53 by the LNER. Between December 1892 and June 1893 ten engines, Nos.921 to 930, were built at Doncaster, all fitted with a 4ft 0$^{1}/_{2}$in. diameter boiler. Nos.921 to 927 had condensing apparatus and worked in London District; the other three were non-condensing and worked in the West Riding. At Grouping, apart from grey paint, they were still almost as built.

The first six engines of Class J54, Nos.494 to 499, were built at Doncaster in 1874 but only No.494 survived unrebuilt to Grouping. It was 29ft 6in. long overall and the bunker only 2ft 6in. long. On 18th July 1923 No.494 went into Doncaster for rebuilding to Class J55, No.496 of this batch having been rebuilt in 1916.

In 1897 Nos.606 (July) and 610 (September) were rebuilt by Ivatt with 4ft 5in. domed boiler and formed the prototype of what became LNER Class J55. No.606 was withdrawn in December 1919 but the other became LNER No.3610A on 5th March 1925 and survived until withdrawn on 27th November 1929. These two engines were from J56 class and no others were similarly dealt with.

ten boilers made in 1917 with experimental iron and steel fireboxes, none were constructed between 1911 and 1925.

Several other types of boiler found their way onto classes J15 and J16 down the years as replacements and exemplifies Doncaster's attitude of 'make do and mend' for its smallest engines. These odd boilers are mentioned later.

By 1923 twenty-eight engines had been converted to Class J16, though withdrawal of J15s also took place before Grouping as were two J16s (including No.606). Under the LNER rebuilding and withdrawal continued side by side, with twenty-three more additions to Class J16 (LNER Class J55). Class J54 became extinct in 1933 and by March 1937 only three J55 remained in service. War extended their life and the last one, in Departmental stock, lasted until July 1950 (No.68319, ex 920).

In addition to the two sizes of boiler used on the Stirling saddle tanks, i.e. 4ft 0½in. diameter domeless on Class J15 (J54) and 4ft 5in. domed on Class J16 (J55), there were a number of odd boilers brought into use to cover shortages at the time or to use up still serviceable boilers, as follows:

4ft 2½in. Diameter Domeless & Domed.

In 1913 two domeless boilers from old Stirling goods engines which had been withdrawn were fitted to Nos.804 and 858. These were of an intermediate size, 4ft 2½in. diameter. No.858 reverted to a normal 4ft 0½in. boiler in 1918, but No.804 received a second 4ft 2½in. domeless boiler in July 1923 off 0-6-0 No.649 (? - *see* table). No.804 was then reclassified J16 and consequently became J55 in 1924 under the LNER scheme. Soon afterwards (*see* below) three other members of Class J54 received previously used 4ft 2½in. *domed* boilers but without reclassification to J55. This anomaly persisted until March 1931 when No.3804 got a 4ft 5in. boiler thus becoming a true J55.

The three engines just referred to were Nos.3679, 3902 and 3906 which received boilers from Stirling 0-4-4 tanks. These were carried to withdrawal.

Boiler No.	*Off engine*	*Onto engine*
484	GNR J7 No.484 1/13w.	804 4/13-4/23.
649	GNR J6 11/18*	804 7/23-2/31
435	GNR J7 1/13#	858 5/13-6/18
1532	G1 No.932 8/24w	3902 4/25-11/30w
6911	G1 No.824 5/19	3906 6/25-10/28w
7130	G1 No.828 11/25w	3679 2/27-1/30w

Key:
w - withdrawal date.
* - boiler 649 may have been used on another engine between 11/18 and its reuse on 804 in 7/23.
# - boiler 435 is believed to have come off engine 481, withdrawn 1/13.

4ft 5in. Domeless

Prior to his death in November 1895, Stirling had drawings prepared for a 4ft 5in. diameter boiler, as usual without a dome. Twenty of these boilers were ordered and fitted to new 0-6-0 tender engines Nos.1021 to 1030 (LNER J7) and 1081 to 1090 (LNER J4) which appeared the following year. Ten more boilers of this type were also constructed as replacements for 4ft 2½in. diameter boilers on Stirling's older 0-6-0s. Thereafter Ivatt adopted the 4ft 5in. boiler as standard for future construction, but with domes.

The ten spare boilers were put to work during 1897-99. Subsequently, due to rotation, a number of the thirty boilers found their way onto other engines, including three 0-4-2s.

Several boilers stood spare for up to six years and during 1923-24 four of these by now elderly boilers were utilised to rebuild Class J54 Nos.494A, 633A, 673 and 3912 to Class J55, introducing a final variation. Three of these engines went to the scrap heap still carrying their domeless boilers, but No.3673 was changed to a domed boiler in June 1927. They could be distinguished by their oval shaped cab front windows and Ivatt pattern smokebox doors.

Boiler No.	*Off engine*	*Onto engine*
724	J4 No.724 3/07*	494A 10/23-8/29w
743	J4 No.743 6/15*	633A 11/23-4/26w
1030	J7 No.1021 1/17, spare	3912 2/24-12/30w
1090	J4 No.1090 1/17, spare	673 12/23-10/26.

Key:
w - withdrawal date
* - boilers 724 and 743 presumably saw further service before going to the 0-6-0Ts.

Class J56 (GNR J17)

The first ten examples of what was to become Stirling's standard 0-6-0 saddle tank were built in 1874/5 (GNR J15). The next ten, Nos.606 to 615, were turned out in 1876/7 and differed in being shorter, with the wheelbase reduced by twelve inches at the rear and the firebox casing shortened from 5ft 6in. to 4ft 10in. The tanks too were 8in. shorter and 3in. narrower. These ten engines were classified J17 and no more were built, all further construction being to Class J15. The reason for this short-lived change in design is not known but may possibly have been introduced to allow these engines to work yards where sharp curves existed.

Down the years the fortune of this small class fluctuated widely. Replacement boilers of the same pattern as the originals were made for five of them, but after the arrival of Ivatt in 1896 no more were constructed because their size was non standard.

Instead, during the following year when Nos.606 and 610 required new boilers, they were extensively reconstructed in order to take the new standard 4ft 5in. diameter domed boiler. This involved lengthening the wheelbase and frames to the 'standard' saddletank dimensions and provision of a new cab, bunker and tank. They were reclassified J16 (LNER J55) and formed the nucleus of the subsequent rebuilds from Class J15 (J54) which began nine years later.

Nos.606 and 610 remained the only such conversions from Class J17, the expense evidently not being considered justified. In 1902 No.614 was scrapped when its original boiler was condemned, but in 1908 No.611 avoided a similar fate when it too needed a new boiler. At that time the domeless boiler from No.162, an old Class J12 4ft 0in. saddletank, became available when this engine was withdrawn. This boiler had the same diameter of 4ft 0½in. but was shorter by seven inches. The other J12 No.166 was scrapped in 1910 and its boiler was similarly fitted to No.613. These short boilers were retained by Nos.611 and 613 to the end.

No.613's old boiler was repaired and put on No.612 in 1911 in which engine it served for another fourteen years. No suitable boilers were available for Nos.607 and 609 and they were scrapped in 1911 and 1914 respectively.

No further reboilerings of the class were necessary until after Grouping at which time there were five survivors,

Nos.608A, 612 and 615 with normal J17 boilers and Nos.611 and 613 with the shorter J12 type, all domeless.

The remaining J17 boilers soon needed to be replaced and in June 1924 No.3615 was given a second hand 4ft 2½in. diameter domed boiler. Several of these had become available as a result of scrapping 0-4-4 tanks. In order to fit Class J56 the firebox casing had to be shortened to 4ft 10in. from 5ft 6in. The dome was retained. No.3608A was similarly dealt with in August 1924 and No.3612 in August 1925. These three boilers saw subsequent use on Class J57 after withdrawal of the J56 class.

Boil No.	*Off class*	*Onto engine*
762	G2 (GN G3) 4/21	3608A 8/24-12/32.
694	G2 (GN G3) 10/24	3612 8/25-10/28.
		On J57 No.3134A 9/29-3/32.
826	G1 12/21	3615 6/24-1/27.
		On J57 No.3149A 1/27-8/31.

With the withdrawal of No.3608A on 8th December 1932, Class J56 became extinct, thirty years after the first withdrawal.

Class J57 (GNR J18)

The design of these eight engines was based on the contemporary batch of GNR Class J15 (LNER J54) saddle tanks and differed principally in having 4ft 0½in. instead of 4ft 8in. wheels and a boiler pitched lower in order to give a very low overall height. This was to enable them to pass beneath the GER main line at Stratford en route to the GN's East London goods depots. At that time the bridge concerned had a headroom of only 11ft 6in.

Eight engines were built at Doncaster in pairs: 1882 - Nos.684 and 685; 1884 - Nos.686 and 687; 1890 - Nos.134 and 140; 1892 - Nos.144 and 149.

The first six had open back cabs but the final two had enclosed cabs in line with current construction of the standard J15 class.

Like the other Stirling saddle tanks, Doncaster fitted these eight engines with a variety of boilers down the years, depending on what was currently available when a fresh boiler was required. Four types of boiler were used.

(a) The original design was domeless, 4ft 0½in. diameter with a barrel 10ft 0in. long. The last one in service on Class J18 was on No.134A until October 1920.

(b) Replacements at first were similar but with 10ft 1in. barrels. Six of the class received these during the period from 1904 to 1912, whilst second hand ones went onto three others.

(c) Standard Ivatt 4ft 5in. diameter boilers with domes were fitted to Nos.685 and 140A in November 1917 whilst No.3134A got one in June 1924 with No.3687 following in October 1928. Wider and higher cabs had to be fitted as well as the saddle tanks having to be altered. No.3134A reverted to type B but retained its bigger cab. Its boiler came from withdrawn No.3686.

(d) A final variety was introduced in January 1927* when No.3149A had its type B boiler replaced by a 4ft 2½in. diameter domed boiler off Class J56 No.3615. This type of boiler had an eight inch shorter firebox and No.3149A had to have its cab lengthened by a like amount. No.3134A also got one of these odd boilers (off J56 No.3612) in September 1929, replacing its previous 4ft 5in. domed boiler (Type C).

** The two boilers referred to here had originated on GNR 0-4-4 tanks of Class G3 (LNER G2) and had been modified for use on Class J56 - q.v.*

Unlike the standard Stirling saddletanks the fitting of larger diameter boilers did not result in any alteration to the class designation either on the GNR or LNER, not even by the use of class parts.

No.3470A (Great Northern Railway Class J19)

This solitary engine had started its life as a saddle tank on the Great Northern Railway in September 1872 after being completely rebuilt at Doncaster works from an ex West Yorkshire Railway Manning, Wardle 1864 built 0-6-0 side tank. Originally numbered 470 by the GN when they took it over in 1865, it was placed on the Duplicate List in 1919 and the suffix 'A' applied.

The boiler carried was a 4ft 0½in. diameter domeless type which had a large fluted cover over the safety valves. This boiler was new in July 1889 and stayed with the engine throughout its life.

In December 1921 No.470A was taken out of Running Stock and put into Service Stock to take up its new employment as shunter for the sleeper depot at Hall Hills. By then it was running as an 0-4-2ST, the rear portion of coupling rods having been detached in 1914 when the engine was converted to burn fuel oil. Previous to its allocation to Boston, it worked as shed pilot at Bowling Junction in Bradford for many years.

Though never classified by the LNER, in January 1925 it was renumbered 3470A during a General overhaul at Doncaster at which time it also received red lining over its black paint. Withdrawal took place in April 1927 when a Sentinel Y1 took over its job at Hall Hills.

3470A

Doncaster 92.

To traffic 9/1872.

REPAIRS:
Don. ?/?—?/7/89.**G**.
Don. 23/10/24—10/1/25.**G**.

BOILERS:
470.
470 *(new)* ?/7/89.

SHEDS:
Boston Sleeper Depot.
To Service Stock 19/12/21.

RENUMBERED:
Duplicate 'A' added 7/7/19.
3470A 10/1/25.

CONDEMNED: 19/4/27.
Cut up at Doncaster.

In 1876/7 Stirling produced at Doncaster a shorter wheelbase version of his standard saddletank which became Class J54. Ten, Nos.606 to 615 were built, but by Grouping only five remained Nos.608A, 611, 612, 613 and 615 and formed Class J56. These were in grey with number on the cab side.

Six engines, numbered 684 to 687, 134 and 140, formed Class J57 and were built at Doncaster during the period from December 1882 to November 1890. They had open cabs, like those which became J54 but their wheels were only 4ft $0^1/_2$in. diameter in place of the 4ft 8in. wheels used on the J54 class. Originally they had a short chimney and a small safety valve cover (*see* page 106, bottom) which were fitted to enable them to clear the 11ft 6in. bridge under the Great Eastern main line at Stratford Low Level. By 1910 that bridge has been raised and standard plain cast chimneys with 11ft 11in. height from rail level were fitted. Note the oval windows due to the original restrictions on cab height.

A saddle tank built at Doncaster in September 1872 had been transferred to Service stock on 19th December 1921 but had retained its number 470A. It worked the sleeper depot at Boston and usually ran without the rear coupling rods. From a General repair, ex works 10th January 1925 it became No.3470A on black paint with single red lining. No LNER classification was allocated to this engine and it was withdrawn on 19th April 1927.

Nos.1251 to 1270, built at Doncaster from December 1901 to March 1902, were generally similar to the others but had raised ventilator with side openings on the cab roof and two-step front footstep with backing plate instead of a single step on a bar.

By Grouping, three had been added to the class by rebuilding from J53 class, Nos.970 (17th December 1921), 977 and 1060 (2nd September 1922). A domed 4ft 5in. boiler replaced the domeless 4ft 0$^{1}/_{2}$in. type hitherto fitted.

CLASS J 52

4201

Doncaster 735.

To Traffic 8/1897.

REPAIRS:
Don. ?/?—?/11/11.**G**.
Don. 4/8—2/12/22.**G**.
Don. 22/5—1/8/25.**G**.
Don. 1/7—17/9/27.**G**.
Don. 18/1—6/3/30.**G**.
Don. 20/2—21/5/32.**G**.
Don. 25/10—17/11/34.**G**.
Don. 25/7—21/8/37.**G**.
Don. 14/5—22/6/40.**G**.
Don. 12/10—6/11/43.**G**.
Don. 15/6—3/8/46.**G**.
Don. 21/9—5/11/49.**G**.
Str. 21/8—20/9/52.**G**.

BOILERS:
1201.
1210 *(ex1210)* ?/11/11.
1314 2/12/22.
7899 *(new)* 17/9/27.
7885 *(ex4218)* 21/8/37.
8522 *(ex3968)* 3/8/46.
8746 *(ex8861)* 5/11/49.
21752 20/9/52.

SHEDS:
Doncaster.
King's Cross 6/3/30.

RENUMBERED:
4201 1/8/25.
8805 9/11/46.
68805 5/11/49.

CONDEMNED: 20/10/55.
Into Don. for cut up 20/10/55.

4202

Doncaster 736.

To Traffic 8/1897.

REPAIRS:
Don. ?/?—?/10/11.**G**.
Don. 17/7—6/10/17.**G**.
Don. 23/1—5/5/23.**G**.
Don. 3/6—25/7/25.**G**.
Don. 1/10/28—5/1/29.**G**.
Don. 22/3—4/7/31.**G**.
Don. 18/6—4/8/34.**G**.
Don. 22/12/36—16/1/37.**G**.
Don. 17/3—10/6/39.**G**.
Don. 7/9—10/10/41.**G**.
Don. 6/4—12/5/44.**G**.
Don. 20/10—16/11/46.**G**.
Don. 1/6—8/7/49.**G**.
Don. 12/6—17/7/52.**G**.

BOILERS:
1202.
1227 *(ex1227)* ?/10/11.
1425 *(exJ4 721)* 5/5/23.
8210 *(new)* 5/1/29.
8423 *(ex4209)* 16/1/37.
8263 *(ex3155A)* 16/11/46.
21648 17/7/52.

SHED:
Doncaster.

RENUMBERED:
4202 25/7/25.
8806 16/11/46.
68806 8/7/49.

CONDEMNED: 31/12/55.
Into Don. for cut up 31/12/55.

4203

Doncaster 737.

To Traffic 9/1897.

REPAIRS:
Don. ?/?—?/7/07.**G**.
Don. ?/?—?/3/16.**G**.
Don. 2/11/18—11/1/19.**G**.
Don. 10/11/23—9/2/24.**G**.
Don. 14/9—15/12/26.**G**.
Don. 1/7—16/11/29.**G**.
Don. 14/9—14/11/31.**G**.
Don. 13/7—25/8/34.**G**.
Don. 12/3—17/4/37.**G**.
Don. 26/9—25/11/39.**G**.
Don. 16/4—3/5/42.**G**.
Don. 25/1—17/3/45.**G**.
Don. 8/6—20/7/47.**G**.
Don. 23/7—13/8/48.**L**.
Don. 12/6—14/7/50.**G**.
Don. 8/3—3/4/53.**G**.

BOILERS:
1203.
1228 *(ex1228)* ?/7/07.
1253 *(ex1253)* ?/3/16.
1285 *(exJ4 354)* 15/12/26.
8341 *(new)* 16/11/29.
8479 *(ex4283 & sp.)* 17/4/37.
8498 *(ex4233 & spare)* 3/5/42.
8339 *(ex8800)* 20/7/47.
10580 *(new)* 14/7/50.
21747 *(ex68853)* 3/4/53.

SHEDS:
Doncaster.
Woodford Halse 31/12/31.
Colwick 21/2/33.
Leicester 10/11/37.
Colwick 8/4/38.

RENUMBERED:
4203 9/2/24.
8807 15/9/46.
68807 13/8/48.

CONDEMNED: 23/9/55.
Into Don. for cut up 23/9/55.

4204

Doncaster 738.

To Traffic 9/1897.

REPAIRS:
Don. ?/?—?/3/09.**G**.
Don. ?/?—?/7/14.**G**.
Don. 3/1—14/2/20.**G**.
Don. 22/2—5/5/23.**G**.
Don. 28/10/25—9/1/26.**G**.
Don. 22/9—3/12/28.**G**.
Don. 18/7—7/11/31.**G**.
Don. 14/6—13/7/35.**G**.
Don. 16/12/38—28/1/39.**G**.
Don. 11/12/42—7/2/43.**G**.
Str. 16/10—30/11/46.**G**.
Str. 19/11—28/12/51.**G**.
Str. 5—21/2/53.**N/C**.

BOILERS:
1204.
1239 *(ex1239)* ?/3/09.
1260 *(ex1260)* ?/7/14.
8205 *(new)* 3/12/28.
8198 *(ex4219)* 30/11/46.
21742 28/12/51.

SHEDS:
King's Cross.
Hornsey 27/3/30.
Ardsley 19/10/52.
Hornsey 23/11/52.

RENUMBERED:
4204 9/1/26.
8808 6/10/46.
68808 28/12/51.

CONDEMNED: 12/4/57.
Into Don. for cut up 12/4/57.

4205

Doncaster 739.

To Traffic 9/1897.

REPAIRS:
Don. 4/10—3/12/21.**G**.
Don. 6/10—13/12/24.**G**.
Don. 13/12/27—3/2/28.**G**.
Don. 20/4—4/10/30.**G**.
Don. 10—24/12/32.**G**.
Don. 14/6—13/7/35.**G**.
Don. 2—22/1/38.**G**.
Don. 11/6—27/7/40.**G**.
Don. 19/4—12/6/43.**G**.
Str. 21/10—24/11/45.**G**.
Str. 15/7—24/8/48.**G**.
Str. 19/12/50—13/1/51.**C/H**.
Str. 5/11—8/12/51.**G**.
Don. 7/9/56. *Not Repaired.*

BOILERS:
1205.
1252 *(ex1252)* 3/12/21
8433 *(new)* 4/10/30.
8204 *(ex4212)* 22/1/38.
8496 *(ex4232)* 24/11/45.
8742 *(ex8832)* 24/8/48.
21725 13/1/51.
21741 8/12/51.

SHEDS:
Trafford Park.
King's Cross 17/4/29.
Spital Bridge 8/2/53.
New England 18/12/55.

RENUMBERED:
4205 13/12/24.
8809 6/10/46.
68809 24/8/48.

CONDEMNED: 11/9/56.
Cut up at Doncaster.

4206

Doncaster 740.

To Traffic 10/1897.

REPAIRS:
Don. 14/3—28/5/21.**G**.
Don. 1/5—30/8/24.**G**.
Don. 19/9—19/11/27.**G**.
Don. 14/10—20/12/30.**G**.
Don. 9/11/33—13/1/34.**G**.
Don. 23/5—20/6/36.**G**.
Don. 21/10—12/11/38.**G**.

(above) **From Grouping, rebuilding from J53 to J52 proceeded steadily and when No.3979 was ex works 2nd November 1932 a further forty-eight had become J52 class, only No.3928 remaining as J53.**

Where condensing gear was fitted, this was not affected by the rebuilding. Note that until at least June 1934, No.3921 still had a GNR District Allocation plate fitted on the cab backplate at top centre; this would be figure 3, No.3921 being in the London District.

No.4052 became J52 when ex works 15th March 1924 whilst it was still shedded at Ardsley and so was not fitted with condensing apparatus.

Nos.4216 to 4225 were built by R.Stephenson & Co. and were the first to have a plate support for the front footsteps, and two steps.

Nos.4251 to 4280 had injectors mounted on the boiler backplate, feeding water directly into the boiler.

About 1928 a start was made on replacing the backplate injectors with a more reliable under-tank injector and on condensing engines they enabled the crosshead pump to be removed.

The cab roof ventilator was added later to a few of the earlier engines, amongst them Nos.4209 and 4238.

4206 cont./
Don. 3/5—7/6/41.**G.**
Don. 27/7—21/8/43.**G.**
Don. 30/1—2/3/46.**G.**
Don. 4/12/47—2/1/48.**G.**
Don. 6/8—13/9/50.**G.**
Don. 29/8—12/9/51.**N/C.**
Don. 19/2—11/3/53.**G.**

BOILERS:
1206.
1123 *(exJ4 352)* 30/8/24.
7982 *(new)* 19/11/27.
8750 *(new)* 20/6/36.
8211 *(ex4253 & sp.)* 21/8/43.
8256 *(ex8786)* 2/1/48.
21620 13/9/50.
21778 *(new)* 11/3/53.

SHEDS:
Trafford Park.
Bidston 20/6/29.
Wrexham ?/?/?.
Gorton 14/10/30.
Colwick 15/12/30.

RENUMBERED:
4206 30/8/24.
8810 29/9/46.
68810 13/9/50.

CONDEMNED: 12/11/55.
Into Don. for cut up 12/11/55.

4207

Doncaster 741.

To Traffic 10/1897.

REPAIRS:
Don. ?/?—?/3/06.**G.**
Don. ?/?—?/5/14.**G.**
Don. 5/7—21/8/20.**G.**
Don. 2/1—19/4/24.**G.**
Don. 29/4—18/6/27.**G.**
Don. 4/1—15/2/30.**G.**
Don. 29/9—25/11/33.**G.**
Don. 10/12/36—23/1/37.**G.**
Don. 3/1—22/2/41.**G.**
Str. 24/1—1/3/46.**G.**
Str. 1—26/3/49.**C/H.**
Str. 15/4—25/5/51.**G.**
Don. 21/5/57. *Not Repaired.*

BOILERS:
1207.
1243 *(ex1243)* ?/3/06.
1259 *(ex1259)* ?/5/14.
7894 *(new)* 18/6/27.
8422 *(ex4264)* 23/1/37.
8654 *(ex4214)* 22/2/41.
7899 *(ex4216)* 1/3/46.
8216 *(ex8791)* 26/3/49.
21733 25/5/51.

SHEDS:
Ardsley.
Hornsey *by* 1/1/35.
Sheffield 19/10/52.
Doncaster 25/1/53.

RENUMBERED:
4207 19/4/24.
8811 3/11/46.
68811 26/3/49.

CONDEMNED: 27/5/57.
Cut up at Doncaster.

4208

Doncaster 742.

To Traffic 10/1897.

REPAIRS:
Don. ?/?—?/7/06.**G.**
Don. ?/?—?/6/16.**G.**
Don. 16/4—28/6/19.**G.**
Don. 8/8—22/11/24.**G.**
Don. 14/9—4/11/27.**G.**
Don. 8/1—28/3/31.**G.**
Don. 19/4—26/5/34.**G.**
Don. 9—28/3/36.**G.**
Don. 21/9—15/10/38.**G.**
Don. 6/2—8/3/41.**G.**
Don. 14/8—5/9/43.**G.**
Don. 2—24/3/45.**G.**
Don. 20/9—20/10/47.**G.**
Don. 28/11—23/12/49.**G.**
Don. 17/7—15/8/52.**G.**

BOILERS:
1208.
1242 *(ex1242)* ?/7/06.
1233 *(ex1239)* ?/6/16.
7981 *(new)* 4/11/27.
Unknown boiler 28/3/31.
8743 *(new)* 26/5/34.
8474 *(ex3961)* 15/10/38.
8210 *(ex3978 & spare)* 5/9/43.
8475 *(ex4288)* 24/3/45.
8347 *(ex68879)* 23/12/49.
21649 15/8/52.

SHED:
Colwick.

RENUMBERED:
4208 22/11/24.
8812 29/9/46.
68812 23/12/49.

CONDEMNED: 16/9/55.
Into Don. for cut up 16/9/55.

4209

Doncaster 743.

To Traffic 10/1897.

REPAIRS:
Don. 29/4—27/8/21.**G.**
Don. 30/1—18/4/25.**G.**
Don. 6/11/27—14/1/28.**G.**
Don. 15/4—7/6/30.**G.**
Don. 3/11—23/12/33.**G.**
Don. 7/11—5/12/36.**G.**
Don. 10/11—30/12/39.**G.**
Don. 17/4—15/5/43.**G.**
Don. 19/11—15/12/45.**G.**
Don. 13—20/7/46.**L.**
Don. 13/5—11/6/48.**G.**
Don. 9/4—1/5/51.**G.**
Don. 16/11—9/12/53.**G.**
Don. 18/5—9/6/54.**C/L.**

BOILERS:
1209.
6985 27/8/21.
8423 *(new)* 7/6/30.
7980 *(ex4231)* 5/12/36.
9158 *(new)* 30/12/39.
21694 *(new)* 1/5/51.

SHEDS:
New England.
Doncaster 31/5/43.

RENUMBERED:
4209 18/4/25.
8813 22/9/46.
68813 11/6/48.

CONDEMNED: 15/10/56.
Into Don. for cut up 15/10/56.

4210

Doncaster 744.

To Traffic 10/1897.

REPAIRS:
Don. ?/?—?/4/10.**G.**
Don. 6/11/22—24/3/23.**G.**
Don. 7/4—25/7/25.**G.**
Don. 22/6—3/8/28.**G.**
Don. 28/3—1/8/31.**G.**
Don. 13/8—22/9/34.**G.**
Don. 4/2—13/3/37.**G.**
Don. 2/3—13/4/40.**G.**
Don. 30/1—20/3/43.**G.**
Don. 14/8—8/9/45.**G.**
Don. 24/11—24/12/47.**G.**
Don. 16/2—6/4/50.**G.**
Don. 14/12/52—8/1/53.**G.**

BOILERS:
1210.
1230 *(ex1230)* ?/4/10.
7086 24/3/23.
8491 *(new)* 1/8/31.
7897 *(ex4227)* 13/3/37.
9155 *(new)* 13/4/40.
9500 *(new)* 8/9/45.
8743 *(ex8768)* 6/4/50.
21779 *(new)* 8/1/53.

SHEDS:
Grantham.
Colwick 22/2/29.
Leicester 10/11/37.
Colwick 27/3/38.

RENUMBERED:
4210 25/7/25.
8814 13/10/46.
68814 6/4/50.

CONDEMNED: 24/11/55.
Into Don. for cut up 24/11/55.

4216

R. Stephenson & Co. 2921.

To Traffic 12/1898.

REPAIRS:
Don. 7/12/21—14/4/22.**G.**
Don. 21/9—5/12/25.**G.**
Don. 7/7—1/9/28.**G.**
Don. 28/6—1/11/30.**G.**
Don. 5/1—31/3/34.**G.**
Don. 20/8—4/9/37.**G.**
Don. 14/6—2/8/41.**G.**
Str. 16/12/45—19/1/46.**G.**
Str. 30/9—2/11/48.**L.**
Str. 9/11—23/12/49.**G.**
Don. 6—26/8/54.**G.**
Don. 27/8—1/9/54.**N/C.**
Don. 15/5/58. *Not Repaired.*

BOILERS:
1216.

WORKS CODES:- Cow - Cowlairs. Dar - Darlington. Don - Doncaster. Ghd - Gateshead. Gor - Gorton. Inv - Inverurie. Kit - Kittybrewster. RSH - Robert, Stephenson & Hawthorn. Str - Stratford. Yk - York.
REPAIR CODES:- **C/H** - Casual Heavy. **C/L** - Casual Light. **G** - General. **H**- Heavy. **H/I** - Heavy Intermediate. **L** - Light. **L/I** - Light Intermediate. **N/C** - Non-Classified.

These cab roof ventilators were added either before or around the time of Grouping.

The last twenty built, Nos.1271 to 1290, had a flared top to the bunker and only two instead of three open coal rails.

Only the last ten engines, Nos.1281 to 1290, built December 1908 to February 1909, had fluted coupling rods, all earlier engines having flat type although there were some later conversions - *see* page 17, bottom.

All except three of the rebuilds from J53 which were fitted for condensing retained that apparatus when they became J52 class.

In February 1932 No.3923 and in March 1935 No.3925 had the condensing apparatus blanked off but it was not removed. Why this was done is obscure because they remained at Hornsey shed until 1952.

Ex works 9th February 1952, No.68795 was the third to have condensing apparatus blanked off and it too was then at Hornsey shed. In September/October 1952 Hornsey sent 68758 (ex3923) to Colwick shed and the other two to Doncaster shed.

Beginning in October 1926 all new boilers were fitted with Ross 'pops' instead of Ramsbottom safety valves - No.4252 was so fitted in June 1930.

4216 cont./
6938 14/4/22.
8658 *(new)* 31/3/34.
7899 *(ex4201)* 4/9/37.
8480 *(ex4252)* 19/1/46.
9644 *(new)* 23/12/49.
21771 *(ex68829)* 26/8/54.

SHEDS:
New England.
Trafford Park 9/12/25.
King's Cross 27/9/28.
Hornsey 28/3/30.
Frodingham 19/10/52.
Grantham 7/12/52.
New England 29/4/56.
Doncaster 29/12/57.

RENUMBERED:
4216 5/12/25.
8815 6/10/46.
68815 2/11/48.

CONDEMNED: 15/5/58.
Cut up at Doncaster.

4217

R. Stephenson & Co. 2922.

To Traffic 1/1899.

REPAIRS:
Don. 30/8—6/12/19.**G**.
Don. 15/3—12/6/23.**G**.
Don. 25/4—9/7/24.**L**.
Don. 15/6—18/8/27.**G**.
Don. 31/1—15/3/30.**G**.
Don. 2/4—3/9/32.**G**.
Don. 1/8—7/9/35.**G**.
Don. 18/8—3/9/38.**G**.
Don. 15/6—12/7/41.**G**.
Don. 8—29/7/44.**G**.
Don. 3/6—10/7/47.**G**.
Don. 22/5/50. *Not Repaired.*
To Service Stock 29/5/50.
Don. ?/4—21/5/51.**G**.
Don. 21—25/6/54.**N/C**.

BOILERS:
1217.
7895 *(new)* 18/8/27.
8425 *(ex4290)* 3/9/38.
8425 reno.S.B.923 29/5/50.
S.B.950 21/5/51.

SHEDS:
Lincoln.
Louth 12/3/28.
Ardsley 22/3/30.
Grantham 26/5/30.
Doncaster Works 29/5/50.

RENUMBERED:
4217 18/8/27.
8816 15/10/46.
68816 21/5/51.
DEPT'L **No. 2** 13/11/52.

WITHDRAWN: 29/5/50.
CONDEMNED: 11/3/56.
Into Don. for cut up 11/3/56.

4218

R. Stephenson & Co. 2923.

To Traffic 2/1899.

REPAIRS:
Don. 18/10/22—31/3/23.**G**.
Don. 9/7—23/12/26.**G**.
Don. 7/12/29—3/1/30.**G**.
Don. 5/5—12/8/33.**G**.
Don. 25/6—25/7/36.**G**.
Don. 25/12/39—10/2/40.**G**.
Don. 2/12/42—30/1/43.**G**.
Don. 19/7—31/8/46.**G**.
Don. 14/9—22/10/48.**G**.
Don. 9—31/7/51.**G**.
Don. 27/3—23/4/54.**G**.
Don. 4/4/58. *Not Repaired.*

BOILERS:
1218.
7885 *(new)* 23/12/26.
7904 *(ex4270)* 25/7/36.
8519 *(ex4254 & sp.)* 30/1/43.
21697 *(new)* 31/7/51.

SHEDS:
New England.
Grantham 12/8/33.
New England 30/8/33.
Spital Bridge 15/5/55.
New England 2/10/55.
Spital Bridge 6/11/55.
New England 4/12/55.
Doncaster 22/4/56.

RENUMBERED:
4218 23/12/26.
8817 29/9/46.
68817 22/10/48.

CONDEMNED: 4/4/58.
Cut up at Doncaster.

4219

R. Stephenson & Co. 2924.

To Traffic 2/1899.

REPAIRS:
Don. 5/8—5/11/21.**G**.
Don. 8/12/24—5/9/25.**G**.
Don. 16/2—27/10/28.**G**.
Don. 24/11/31—6/2/32.**G**.
Don. 13/7—25/8/34.**G**.
Don. 15/3—22/5/37.**G**.
Don. 14/1—23/3/40.**G**.
Don. 13/12/43—15/1/44.**G**.
Don. 15/8—20/9/46.**G**.
Str. 15/10—3/12/49.**G**.
Don. 29/11—23/12/52.**G**.

BOILERS:
1219.
6916 *(exJ4 1154)* 5/9/25.
8198 *(new)* 27/10/28.
8343 *(ex3927)* 20/9/46.
9642 *(new)* 3/12/49.
21657 23/12/52.

SHEDS:
New England.
King's Cross 16/4/35.

RENUMBERED:
4219 5/9/25.
8818 20/9/46.
68818 3/12/49.

CONDEMNED: 16/11/55.
Into Don. for cut up 16/11/55.

4220

R. Stephenson & Co. 2925.

To Traffic 2/1899.

REPAIRS:
Don. 27/10—20/12/19.**G**.
Don. 27/9/22—13/1/23.**G**.
Don. 28/10/25—13/2/26.**G**.
Don. 6/5—20/7/29.**G**.
Don. 17/9—17/12/32.**G**.
Don. 16/10—23/11/35.**G**.
Don. 18/1—11/2/39.**G**.
Don. 5/1—15/2/42.**G**.
Don. 15/4—19/5/45.**G**.
Don. 29/12/47—28/1/48.**G**.
Don. 28/10—17/11/50.**H/I**.
Don. 11/5—10/6/53.**G**.

BOILERS:
1220.
1624 *(exG1 770)* 13/2/26.
6937 *(ex3970)* 20/7/29.
8653 *(new)* 17/12/32.
8653 reno.21625 17/11/50.
21673 10/6/53.

SHEDS:
New England.
Hitchin 26/9/54.
New England 30/1/55.
Colwick 9/10/55.

RENUMBERED:
4220 13/2/26.
8819 22/9/46.
E8819 28/1/48.
68819 17/11/50.

CONDEMNED: 18/6/56.
Into Don. for cut up 18/6/56.

4221

R. Stephenson & Co. 2926.

To Traffic 3/1899.

REPAIRS:
Don. 10/5—29/7/22.**G**.
Don. 29/6—29/8/25.**G**.
Don. 3/3—11/5/28.**G**.
Don. 11/11/30—21/2/31.**G**.
Don. 7/12/33—26/2/34.**G**.
Don. 2/4—2/5/36.**G**.
Don. 16/12/38—14/1/39.**G**.
Don. 30/4—7/6/41.**G**.
Don. 3—25/3/44.**G**.
Don. 11/8—3/10/47.**G**.
Don. 1/4—5/5/50.**G**.
Don. 7/11—3/12/52.**G**.

BOILERS:
1221.
1681 *(ex1274)* 29/7/22.
8477 *(new)* 21/2/31.
9500 *(ex8814)* 5/5/50.
21655 3/12/52.

SHED:
New England.

RENUMBERED:
4221 29/8/25.
8820 28/10/46.
68820 5/5/50.

CONDEMNED: 16/12/55.
Into Don. for cut up 16/12/55.

4222

R. Stephenson & Co. 2927.

To Traffic 3/1899.

REPAIRS:
Don. 4/8—29/10/21.**G**.
Don. 18/9—5/12/25.**G**.
Don. 23/10—14/12/28.**G**.
Don. 4/6—5/11/32.**G**.
Don. 29/6—10/8/35.**G**.
Don. 5/1—4/2/39.**G**.
Don. 8/9—2/11/41.**G**.
Don. 15/7—5/8/44.**G**.
Don. 21/9—10/10/47.**G**.

4222 cont./
Don. 23/8—22/9/50.**G.**
Don. 8/6—15/7/53.**G.**

BOILERS:
1222.
1656 *(exJ4 1106)* 29/10/21.
8208 *(new)* 14/12/28.
21622 22/9/50.
21674 15/7/53.

SHEDS:
New England.
Colwick 7/11/54.

RENUMBERED:
4222 5/12/25.
8821 10/11/46.
68821 22/9/50.

CONDEMNED: 14/3/56.
Into Don. for cut up 14/3/56.

4223

R. Stephenson & Co. 2928.

To Traffic 4/1899.

REPAIRS:
Don. 21/7—16/10/20.**G.**
Don. 26/2—23/5/25.**G.**
Don. 10/6—27/8/27.**G.**
Don. 27/1—15/3/30.**G.**
Don. 19/3—2/7/32.**G.**
Don. 18/8—22/9/34.**G.**
Don. 12/2—20/3/37.**G.**
Don. 12/8—21/9/40.**G.**
Don. 13/9—7/10/44.**G.**
Str. 19/8—5/10/47.**G.**
Str. 9/5—17/6/50.**G.**
Don. 5/2—14/4/53.**G.**

BOILERS:
1223.
7892 *(new)* 27/8/27.
8745 *(new)* 22/9/34.
8436 *(ex4260)* 7/10/44.
8518 *(ex8874)* 17/6/50.
21667 14/4/53.

SHEDS:
New England.
King's Cross 22/3/30.

RENUMBERED:
4223 23/5/25.
8822 20/7/46.
68822 17/6/50.

CONDEMNED: 11/10/56.
Into Don. for cut up 11/10/56.

4224

R. Stephenson & Co. 2929.

To Traffic 4/1899.

REPAIRS:
Don. 26/7—20/11/22.**G.**
Don. 5/10—19/12/25.**G.**
Don. 14/5—6/7/29.**G.**
Don. 17/9—19/11/32.**G.**
Don. 26/7—24/8/35.**G.**
Don. 11/11—3/12/38.**G.**
Don. 2/2—23/3/42.**G.**
Don. 4/5—9/6/45.**G.**
Don. 9/2—27/2/48.**G.**
Don. 30/1—23/2/51.**G.**
Don. 5/10—5/11/53.**H/I.**
Don. 21/6/57. *Not Repaired.*

BOILERS:
1224.
6935 *(ex1281)* 20/11/22.
8264 *(new)* 6/7/29.
21629 23/2/51.

SHEDS:
New England.
Doncaster 24/3/57.

RENUMBERED:
4224 19/12/25.
8823 17/11/46.
E8823 27/2/48.
68823 23/2/51.

CONDEMNED: 24/6/57.
Cut up at Doncaster.

4225

R. Stephenson & Co. 2930.

To Traffic 4/1899.

REPAIRS:
Don. 7—29/11/19.**L.**
Don. 3/1—22/5/23.**G.**
Don. 9/7—18/12/26.**G.**
Don. 26/2—20/6/30.**G.**
Don. 16/6—26/8/33.**G.**
Don. 16/5—14/6/36.**G.**
Don. 10/7—16/9/39.**G.**
Don. 11/11—12/12/42.**G.**
Don. 10/3—20/4/46.**G.**
Don. 1—25/3/49.**G.**
Don. 5—27/11/51.**G.**
Don. 4/4—4/5/55.**G.**
Don. 16/5—14/6/57.**C/L.**
Don. 20/5/59. *Not Repaired.*

BOILERS:
1225.
1253 *(ex4203)* 18/12/26.
8425 *(new)* 20/6/30.
8202 *(ex4250)* 14/6/36.
8350 *(ex4058)* 16/9/39.
10512 *(new)* 25/3/49.
10512 reno.21636 27/11/51.

SHEDS:
New England.
Hornsey 6/9/53.
Ardsley 5/4/59.

RENUMBERED:
4225 18/12/26.
8824 17/11/46.
68824 25/3/49.

CONDEMNED: 27/5/59.
Cut up at Doncaster.

4226

Sharp Stewart & Co. 4471.

To Traffic 4/1899.

REPAIRS:
Don. ?/?—?/5/06.**G.**
Don. 27/8—25/11/22.**G.**
Don. 27/7—5/9/25.**G.**
Don. 10/1—26/10/28.**G.**
Don. 7/3—18/6/32.**G.**
Don. 9/8—28/9/35.**G.**
Don. 7/2—20/4/40.**G.**
Don. 17/11—27/12/44.**G.**
Don. 22/12/48—9/2/49.**G.**
Str. 10—29/12/51.**C/L.**
Don. 1/8/53. *Not Repaired.*

BOILERS:
1226.
1231 *(ex1231)* ?/5/06.
1165 25/11/22.
8197 *(new)* 26/10/28.
9159 *(new)* 20/4/40.
8651 *(ex8781)* 9/2/49.
8651 reno.21745 29/12/51.

SHEDS:
Ardsley.
Hornsey 31/5/24.
Annesley 19/10/52.
Hornsey 23/11/52.

RENUMBERED:
4226 12/3/25.
8825 10/8/46.
68825 9/2/49.

CONDEMNED: 10/8/53.
Cut up at Doncaster.

4227

Sharp Stewart & Co. 4472.

To Traffic 4/1899.

REPAIRS:
Don. ?/?—?/10/10.**G.**
Don. 30/3—4/6/21.**G.**
Don. 7/7—27/9/24.**G.**
Don. 9/5—2/8/27.**G.**
Don. 8/2—15/3/30.**G.**
Don. 29/9—25/11/33.**G.**
Don. 30/12/36—30/1/37.**G.**
Don. 16/1—8/2/41.**G.**
Don. 17/7—25/8/45.**G.**
Str. 24/5—31/7/48.**L.**
Str. 15/1—25/2/50.**G.**
Don. 20/7—21/8/53.**G.**
Don. 6/3/57. *Not Repaired.*

BOILERS:
1227.
1246 *(ex1246 & sp.)* ?/10/10.
7897 *(new)* 2/8/27.
7894 *(ex4207)* 30/1/37.
8657 *(ex3966)* 25/8/45.
8480 *(ex68815)* 25/2/50.
21675 21/8/53.

SHEDS:
Hornsey.
New England 31/8/52.
Colwick 16/1/55.

RENUMBERED:
4227 27/9/24.
8826 24/11/46.
68826 31/7/48.

CONDEMNED: 11/3/57.
Cut up at Doncaster.

4228

Sharp Stewart & Co. 4473.

To Traffic 4/1899.

REPAIRS:
Don. ?/?—?/11/06.**G.**
Don. 19/3—22/5/20.**G.**
Don. 31/1—21/4/23.**G.**
Don. 16/9—28/11/25.**G.**
Don. 9/11/28—11/5/29.**G.**
Don. 6/2—28/5/32.**G.**
Don. 3/1—15/2/36.**G.**
Don. 12/9—12/10/40.**G.**
Don. 28/10—18/11/44.**G.**
Str. 22/6—30/8/49.**G.**
Don. 2/3—2/4/53.**G.**

BOILERS:
1228.

Starting in 1931 the open coal rails had plating put behind them to help stop spillage of small coal.

Used almost entirely as shunting engines, all except the last two built as J53 (Nos.111 and 155) had 6in. thick wooden buffer beams sandwiched between steel plates fitted at both ends.

(below) **These sandwich type buffer beams survived the rebuilding and Nos.68757 to 68802 kept them to withdrawal.**

(above) **On Nos.111, 155 and all those built as J52, the front buffer beam was $1^{1}/_{2}$in. steel plate with additional 1in. strengthened plate at each end, but the usual sandwich type was fitted at the back.**

Three types of buffers were used, two GNR type and one LNER. By far the majority had this style of parallel shank and circular flange, which most retained to withdrawal.

The earlier GNR design with tapered shank and end collar, could also be seen, fourteen examples having been noted. The only semblance of pattern seems to show Nos.1251 to 1260 were so equipped although No.4252 later changed to parallel shank - ***see*** **page 8, top, and page 11, 2nd top.**

Only one, No.8828 (ex4229) was noted as changed to Group Standard buffers and the date of change is unknown but it had them when ex Stratford works 29th December 1947. Note it has carriage heating equipment with connection also at the front. In 1934 six - Nos.3978, 4216, 4223, 4229, 4234 and 4235 - were so fitted - three King's Cross and three Hornsey allocated engines.

(above) **From 1935 a rectangular opening was cut into the cab splasher plate to give a better toe-hold than the 3in. wide angle iron provided.**

This toe hold was then applied generally to all the class whether condensing or not.

4228 cont./
1208 *(ex1208)* ?/11/06.
1235 *(ex1232)* 22/5/20.
8255 *(new)* 11/5/29.
8431 *(ex4213)* 15/2/36.
8659 *(ex8785)* 30/8/49.
21666 2/4/53.

SHEDS:
Hornsey.
King's Cross 25/11/51.

RENUMBERED:
4228 13/2/25 *at shed.*
8827 8/12/46.
68827 30/8/49.

CONDEMNED: 3/1/56.
Into Don. for cut up 3/1/56.

4229

Sharp Stewart & Co. 4474.

To Traffic 4/1899.

REPAIRS:
Don. ?/?—?/7/06.**G**.
Don. 25/4—30/7/21.**G**.
Don. 30/10/24—11/4/25.**G**.
Don. 21/2—30/7/28.**G**.
Don. 21/3—25/7/31.**G**.
Don. 24/11/33—3/2/34.**G**.
Don. 2/9—3/10/36.**G**.
Don. 5—20/7/40.**G**.
Don. 17/6—29/7/44.**G**.
Str. 8/11—29/12/47.**G**.
Str. 20/11—30/12/50.**G**.
Str. 30/10—3/12/53.**G**.
Don. 17/1/58. *Not Repaired.*

BOILERS:
1229.
1244 *(ex1244)* ?/7/06.
1241 *(ex1230)* 11/4/25.
8492 *(new)* 25/7/31.
8428 *(ex8787)* 29/12/47.
21723 30/12/50.
21676 3/12/53.

SHEDS:
Hornsey.
King's Cross 27/3/30.
New England 22/7/51.
Doncaster 29/12/57.

RENUMBERED:
4229 11/4/25.
8828 15/11/46.
68828 30/12/50.

CONDEMNED: 3/2/58.
Cut up at Doncaster.

4230

Sharp Stewart & Co. 4475.

To Traffic 4/1899.

REPAIRS:
Don. ?/?—?/2/10.**G**.
Don. 2/2—20/5/22.**G**.
Don. 27/10/24—17/1/25.**G**.
Don. 15/10—3/12/27.**G**.
Don. 24/5—26/7/30.**G**.
Don. 16/2—28/4/34.**G**.
Don. 23/6—17/7/37.**G**.
Don. 23/5—15/6/40.**G**.
Don. 22/10—11/12/43.**G**.
Str. 12/11—28/12/46.**G**.
Str. 19/12/47—10/2/48.**G**.
Str. 23/8—29/9/51.**G**.
Don. 15/7—13/8/54.**G**.
Don. 18—21/8/54.**N/C**.
Don. 20/1/58. *Not Repaired.*

BOILERS:
1230.
1241 *(ex1241)* ?/2/10.
6886 *(exE1 1069)* 17/1/25.
8744 *(new)* 28/4/34.
7885 *(ex4201)* 28/12/46.
8213 *(ex8338)* 10/2/48.
21771 *(new)* 29/9/51.
21691 *(ex68837)* 13/8/54.

SHEDS:
Hornsey.
King's Cross 27/5/36.
Hatfield 16/1/43.
Hornsey 19/9/44.
King's Cross 25/11/51.
Colwick 5/8/56.

RENUMBERED:
4230 17/1/25.
8829 7/12/46.
E8829 10/2/48.
68829 29/9/51.

CONDEMNED: 10/2/58.
Cut up at Doncaster.

4231

Sharp Stewart & Co. 4476.

To Traffic 4/1899.

REPAIRS:
Don. ?/?—?/1/06.**G**.
Don. 17/6—7/8/20.**G**.
Don. 30/4—30/8/24.**G**.
Don. 25/8—29/10/27.**G**.
Don. 7/4—6/6/30.**G**.
Don. 11/8—4/11/33.**G**.
Don. 2—24/10/36.**G**.
Don. 13/10—16/12/39.**G**.
Don. 25/9—13/11/43.**G**.
Str. 14/6—17/8/46.**G**.
Str. 3/10—3/11/48.**G**.
Str. 10/1—18/2/50.**G**.
Don. 8/2—3/3/53.**G**.

BOILERS:
1231.
1646 *(new)* ?/1/06.
7980 *(new)* 29/10/27.
8352 *(ex3962)* 24/10/36.
7891 *(ex4215)* 13/11/43.
6879 *(ex3974)* 17/8/46.
8745 *(ex8758)* 3/11/48.
8346 *(ex8770)* 18/2/50.
21663 3/3/53.

SHEDS:
Hornsey.
King's Cross 27/2/35.

RENUMBERED:
4231 30/8/24.
8830 15/11/46.
68830 3/11/48.

CONDEMNED: 13/7/56.
Into Don. for cut up 13/7/56.

4232

Sharp Stewart & Co. 4477.

To Traffic 4/1899.

REPAIRS:
Don. ?/?—?/2/07.**G**.
Don. ?/?—?/11/19.**G**.
Don. 2/8—19/12/22.**G**.
Don. 12/5—18/7/25.**G**.
Don. 12/7—6/11/28.**G**.
Don. 27/6—19/9/31.**G**.
Don. 27/10—23/12/33.**G**.
Don. 24/6—11/7/36.**G**.
Don. 5/3—22/4/39.**G**.
Don. 2—24/12/42.**G**.
Str. 24/7—22/9/45.**G**.
Str. 25/9—17/11/48.**G**.
Str. 12/9—3/11/51.**G**.
Don. 11/11—10/12/54.**G**.
Don. 13—15/12/24.**N/C**.
Don. 20/1/59. *Not Repaired.*

BOILERS:
1232.
1235 *(ex1235)* ?/2/07.
1237 *(ex1237)* ?/11/19.
8496 *(new)* 19/9/31.
8344 *(ex4054)* 22/9/45.
21739 3/11/51.
21640 *(ex68844)* 10/12/54.

SHEDS:
Hornsey.
King's Cross 29/3/30.
Spital Bridge 8/2/53.
Grantham 14/2/54.
New England 29/4/56.
King's Cross 24/3/57.

RENUMBERED:
4232 18/7/25.
8831 27/10/46.
68831 17/11/48.

CONDEMNED: 20/1/59.
Cut up at Doncaster.

4233

Sharp Stewart & Co. 4478.

To Traffic 4/1899.

REPAIRS:
Don. ?/?—?/9/06.**G**.
Don. ?/?—?/1/19.**G**.
Don. ?/?—?/3/20.**G**.
Don. 27/9/21—17/1/22.**G**.
Don. 26/3—13/6/25.**G**.
Don. 11/7—3/11/28.**G**.
Don. 14/12/31—30/1/32.**G**.
Don. 17/5—15/6/35.**G**.
Don. 11/6—27/7/40.**G**.
Don. 4/9—26/10/40.**H**.
Str. 4/4—5/5/45.**G**.
Str. 12/4—26/6/48.**G**.
Str. 22/1—24/2/51.**G**.
Don. 5—28/1/54.**G**.
Don. 16/10/57. *Not Repaired.*

BOILERS:
1233.
1226 *(ex1226)* ?/9/06.
1247 ?/1/19.
8498 *(new)* 30/1/32.
8742 *(ex4283)* 26/10/40.
8321 *(ex8802)* 26/6/48.
21726 24/2/51.
21679 28/1/54.

SHEDS:
Hornsey.
King's Cross 14/9/42.

RENUMBERED:
4233 13/6/25.
8832 24/11/46.
68832 26/6/48.

CONDEMNED: 21/10/57.
Cut up at Doncaster.

(above) **By Grouping, two steps had been fitted on the right hand side of the bunker, but not on the left hand side.**

The left hand side of the bunker remained without any access steps through to withdrawal.

(below) **From January 1937 to March 1938 No.4242 was fitted with a Sentinel mechanical stoker. It was the only one so equipped and it never operated outside the Doncaster Plant works.**

4234

Sharp Stewart & Co. 4479.

To Traffic 4/1899.

REPAIRS:
Don. 14/12/21—25/3/22.**G.**
Don. 16/1—7/3/25.**G.**
Don. 21/12/27—24/2/28.**G.**
Don. 29/8—12/10/31.**G.**
Don. 13/9—19/10/35.**G.**
Don. 2/9—22/10/39.**G.**
Don. 20/6—22/7/44.**G.**
Str. 25/11—31/12/48.**G.**
Don. 12/7—7/8/53.**G.**
Don. 2/2/56. *Not Repaired.*

BOILERS:
1234.
1627 25/3/22.
8494 *(new)* 12/10/31.
9496 *(ex8889)* 3/12/48.
21720 *(ex68838)* 7/8/53.

SHEDS:
Hornsey.
Doncaster 19/10/52.
Mexborough 18/4/54.

RENUMBERED:
4234 7/3/25.
8833 3/11/46.
68833 31/12/48.

CONDEMNED: 20/2/56.
Cut up at Doncaster.

4235

Sharp Stewart & Co. 4480.

To Traffic 4/1899.

REPAIRS:
Don. ?/?—?/7/06.**G.**
Don. ?/?—?/11/10.**G.**
Don. 4/10—24/12/21.**G.**
Don. 18/7—6/9/24.**G.**
Don. 4/8—14/10/27.**G.**
Don. 28/6—11/10/30.**G.**
Don. 5/1—7/4/34.**G.**
Don. 16—28/8/37.**G.**
Don. 5/4—17/5/41.**G.**
Str. 3/1—2/2/46.**G.**
Str. 6/12/49—21/1/50.**G.**
Don. 2—31/12/54.**G.**
Don. 6/2/60. *Not Repaired.*

BOILERS:
1235.
1207 *(ex1207)* ?/7/06.
1204 *(ex1204)* ?/11/10.
1259 *(ex4207)* 14/10/27.
8435 *(new)* 11/10/30.
8346 *(ex4049)* 28/8/37.
8204 *(ex4205)* 2/2/46.
8343 *(ex8818)* 21/1/50.
21646 *(ex68839)* 31/12/54.

SHEDS:
Hornsey.
Doncaster 19/10/52.
Hornsey 23/11/52.
Ardsley 8/2/59.

RENUMBERED:
4235 6/9/24.
8834 6/10/46.
68834 21/1/50.

CONDEMNED: 22/2/60.
Cut up at Doncaster.

4236

Sharp Stewart & Co. 4481.

To Traffic 4/1899.

REPAIRS:
Don. ?/?—?/9/14.**G.**
Don. 15/11/21—28/3/22.**G.**
Don. 5/5—25/7/25.**G.**
Don. 1/10—28/12/28.**G.**
Don. 8/11/30—24/1/31.**G.**
Don. 2—30/9/33.**G.**
Don. 28/3—25/4/36.**G.**
Don. 25/9—15/10/38.**G.**
Don. 3—22/2/41.**G.**
Don. 18/12/43—1/1/44.**G.**
Don. 17/4—8/6/46.**G.**
Don. 13/11—17/12/48.**G.**
Don. 14/11—10/12/51.**G.**
Don. 7/12/54—7/1/55.**G.**
Don. 26/1/58. *Not Repaired.*

BOILERS:
1236.
1261 *(ex1261)* ?/9/14.
8211 *(new)* 28/12/28.
7987 *(ex4245)* 25/4/36.
8440 *(ex8867)* 17/12/48.
21638 10/12/51.
21644 *(ex68846)* 7/1/55.

SHED:
Doncaster.

RENUMBERED:
4236 25/7/25.
8835 3/11/46.
68835 17/12/48.

CONDEMNED: 10/2/58.
Cut up at Doncaster.

4237

Sharp Stewart & Co. 4482.

To Traffic 4/1899.

REPAIRS:
Don. ?/?—?/8/18.**G.**
Don. 15/8—16/12/22.**G.**
Don. 5/5—4/7/25.**G.**
Don. 16/3—14/8/28.**G.**
Don. 15/9—6/12/30.**G.**
Don. 5/6—26/8/33.**G.**
Don. 8/3—4/4/36.**G.**
Don. 17/7—13/8/38.**G.**
Don. 7—25/1/41.**G.**
Don. 3—24/12/43.**G.**
Don. 20/8—5/10/46.**G.**
Don. 14/4—2/5/48.**L.**
Don. 24/5—16/6/49.**G.**
Don. 14/8—15/9/52.**G.**
Don. 20—27/3/53.**N/C.**
Don. 2/10/56. *Not Repaired.*

BOILERS:
1237.
1680 *(ex1278 & spare)* ?/8/18.
8440 *(new)* 6/12/30.
8258 *(ex4215)* 13/8/38.
10513 *(new)* 16/6/49.
21651 15/9/52.

SHED:
Doncaster.

RENUMBERED:
4237 4/7/25.
8836 5/10/46.
68836 1/5/48.

CONDEMNED: 3/10/56.
Cut up at Doncaster.

4238

Sharp Stewart & Co. 4483.

To Traffic 4/1899.

REPAIRS:
Don. ?/?—?/11/07.**G.**
Don. ?/?—?/6/15.**G.**
Don. 9/2—1/5/20.**G.**
Don. 11/2—28/6/24.**G.**
Don. 31/3—25/5/27.**G.**
Don. 19/11—31/12/29.**G.**
Don. 29/12/31—5/3/32.**G.**
Don. 28/2—22/4/33.**G.**
Don. 27/2—23/3/35.**G.**
Don. 4—27/11/37.**G.**
Don. 29/5—22/6/40.**G.**
Don. 4—31/7/43.**G.**
Don. 2/2—9/3/46.**G.**
Don. 30/7—27/8/48.**G.**
Don. 5—27/2/51.**G.**
Don. 1—28/7/54.**G.**
Don. 19/2/59. *Not Repaired.*

BOILERS:
1238.
1232 *(ex1232)* ?/11/07.
1236 *(ex1236)* ?/6/15.
7898 *(new)* 25/5/27.
8748 *(new)* 23/3/35.
9811 *(new)* 27/8/48.
21691 *(new)* 27/2/51.
21736 *(ex68862)* 28/7/54.

SHED:
Doncaster.

RENUMBERED:
4238 28/6/24.
8837 28/4/46.
68837 27/8/48.

CONDEMNED: 23/2/59.
Cut up at Doncaster.

4239

Sharp Stewart & Co. 4484.

To Traffic 4/1899.

REPAIRS:
Don. ?/?—?/4/07.**G.**
Don. ?/?—?/6/15.**G.**
Don. 3/8—16/12/22.**G.**
Don. 20/4—4/7/25.**G.**
Don. 8/8/28—12/1/29.**G.**
Don. 5/1—21/3/31.**G.**
Don. 17/3—19/5/34.**G.**
Don. 28/9—24/10/36.**G.**
Don. 11/11/39—6/1/40.**G.**
Don. 1/12/43—15/1/44.**G.**
Str. 10/9—2/11/47.**G.**
Str. 21/10—22/11/49.**C/L.**
Str. 9/8—16/9/50.**G.**
Don. 6/7—6/8/53.**G.**

BOILERS:
1239.
1233 *(ex1233)* ?/4/07.
1263 *(ex1263)* ?/6/15.
8212 *(new)* 12/1/29.
8213 *(ex4253)* 24/10/36.
8345 *(ex8856)* 2/11/47.
21720 16/9/50.
21622 *(ex68821)* 6/8/53.

SHEDS:
Doncaster.
King's Cross 19/5/34.

RENUMBERED:
4239 4/7/25.
8838 27/7/46.

Although the leading and middle wheel splashers had brass beading around their edge, by 1923 this was usually painted over. For years Hornsey shed kept one of their allocation particularly clean and when No.4252 filled that role, its splasher beadings were kept highly polished.

Some of the condenser-fitted engines worked though to Southern Railway goods yards and had extra lamp brackets so that they could display SR lamp codes to indicate class of train and route.

The first ten built as J52, Nos.4201 to 4210, originally had plain chimneys 3ft 3in. high but by Grouping a built-up type had replaced them.

4239 cont./
68838 16/9/50.

CONDEMNED: 7/8/56.
Into Don. for cut up 7/8/56.

4240

Sharp Stewart & Co. 4485.

To Traffic 4/1899.

REPAIRS:
Don. 27/10—6/12/19.**G.**
Don. 6/6—1/9/23.**G.**
Don. 29/10/25—27/2/26.**G.**
Don. 29/10/28—29/1/29.**G.**
Don. 9/3—11/6/32.**G.**
Don. 4—30/3/35.**G.**
Don. 12—30/10/37.**G.**
Don. 31/3—4/5/40.**G.**
Don. 10/12/42—2/1/43.**G.**
Don. 20/2—24/3/45.**G.**
Don. 7/8—25/9/47.**G.**
Don. 1/8—1/9/49.**G.**
Don. 25/2—25/3/52.**G.**
Don. 25/11—22/12/54.**G.**
Don. 20—23/7/56.**N/C.**
Don. 8/4/58. *Not Repaired.*

BOILERS:
1240.
1203 *(ex1258)* 6/12/19.
6887 *(ex D4 4079)* 27/2/26.
8216 *(new)* 29/1/29.
7983 *(ex3966)* 30/3/35.
8261 *(ex4266)* 30/10/37.
7980 *(ex4209)* 4/5/40.
8257 *(ex4242 & spare)* 2/1/43.
8474 *(ex4208 & sp.)* 24/3/45.
8212 *(ex8841)* 1/9/49.
21646 25/3/52.
21731 *(ex68764)* 22/12/54.

SHEDS:
King's Cross.
Gorton 17/3/26.
Colwick 26/1/29.
Leicester ?/9/52.

RENUMBERED:
1240N 1/9/23.
4240 27/2/26.
8839 24/11/46.
68839 1/9/49.

CONDEMNED: 8/4/58.
Cut up at Doncaster.

4241

Sharp Stewart & Co. 4486.

To Traffic 5/1899.

REPAIRS:
Don. ?/?—?/2/07.**G.**
Don. ?/?—?/5/14.**G.**
Don. 31/3—22/5/20.**G.**
Don. 11/8—8/11/24.**G.**
Don. 17/2—12/5/27.**G.**
Don. 17/12/29—8/2/30.**G.**
Don. 5/12/31—20/2/32.**G.**
Don. 28/1—6/5/33.**G.**
Don. 28/2—28/3/36.**G.**
Don. 29/3—20/5/39.**G.**
Don. 17/2—9/5/42.**G.**
Don. 6—29/9/45.**G.**
Don. 29/2—8/4/48.**G.**
Don. 21/3—16/4/51.**G.**
Don. 1—26/2/54.**G.**
Don. 9/1/58. *Not Repaired.*
To Service Stock 27/1/58.

BOILERS:
1241.
1229 *(ex1229)* ?/2/07.
1201 *(ex1201 & spare)* ?/5/14.
1438 *(ex J4 334)* 8/11/24.
8324 *(new)* 8/2/30.
21693 *(new)* 16/4/51.
21693 reno.S.B.1112 27/1/58.

SHEDS:
Doncaster.
King's Cross 21/5/27.
New England 2/5/33.
Doncaster 24/3/57.
Doncaster Works 27/1/58.

RENUMBERED:
4241 8/11/24.
8840 28/7/46.
68840 8/4/48.
DEPT'L No. 9 27/1/58.

WITHDRAWN: 27/1/58.
CONDEMNED: 3/2/61.
Into Don. for cut up 3/2/61.

4242

Sharp Stewart & Co. 4487.

To Traffic 5/1899.

REPAIRS:
Don. ?/?—?/2/06.**G.**
Don. 1/5—29/6/18.**G.**
Don. 14/7—8/9/23.**G.**
Don. 15/4—24/7/26.**G.**
Don. 5/12/28—1/6/29.**G.**
Don. 27/8—10/10/31.**G.**
Don. 6/8—8/9/34.**G.**
Don. 22/11/36—9/1/37.**G.**
Automatic stoker fitted.
Auto stoker removed 3/38.
Don. 2—20/7/40.**G.**
Don. 4/11—4/12/43.**G.**
Don. 27/5—6/7/46.**G.**
Don. 21/2—11/3/49.**G.**
Don. 24/3—24/4/52.**H/I.**
Don. 25/3/57. *Not Repaired.*

BOILERS:
1242.
1643 *(new)* ?/2/06.
1242 *(ex1208)* 29/6/18.
8257 *(new)* 1/6/29.
8212 *(ex3966)* 20/7/40.
8751 *(ex8849)* 11/3/49.
8751 reno. 21647 24/4/52.

SHED:
Doncaster.

RENUMBERED:
1242N 8/9/23.
4242 24/7/26.
8841 29/9/46.
68841 11/3/49.

CONDEMNED: 1/4/57.
Cut up at Doncaster.

4243

Sharp Stewart & Co. 4488.

To Traffic 5/1899.

REPAIRS:
Don. ?/?—?/11/05.**G.**
Don. 1/6—15/10/21.**G.**
Don. 17/4—13/6/25.**G.**
Don. 17/3—14/8/28.**G.**
Don. 18/7—8/11/30.**G.**
Don. 26/5—26/8/33.**G.**
Don. 3—28/3/36.**G.**
Don. 7—30/7/38.**G.**
Don. 28/11—28/12/40.**G.**
Don. 9/9—3/10/43.**G.**
Don. 2—29/3/46.**G.**
Don. 3/11—3/12/48.**G.**
Don. 14/7—9/8/51.**G.**
Don. 19/3—18/4/55.**G.**
Don. 20—22/4/55.**N/C.**
Don. 26/7/58. *Not Repaired.*

BOILERS:
1243.
1645 *(new)* ?/11/05.
1434 *(exJ4 304)* 15/10/21.
8439 *(new)* 8/11/30.
7887 *(ex4047)* 30/7/38.
9815 *(new)* 3/12/48.
21698 *(new)* 9/8/51.
21639 *(ex68848)* 18/4/55.

SHEDS:
Doncaster.
Retford 11/9/55.
Doncaster 16/10/55.

RENUMBERED:
4243 13/6/25.
8842 29/3/46.
68842 3/12/48.

CONDEMNED: 26/7/58.
Cut up at Doncaster.

4244

Sharp Stewart & Co. 4489.

To Traffic 5/1899.

REPAIRS:
Don. ?/?—?/11/05.**G.**
Don. ?/?—?/6/16.**G.**
Don. 14/6—23/8/19.**G.**
Don. 11/8—1/11/24.**G.**
Don. 16/6—30/8/27.**G.**
Don. 9/11—14/12/29.**G.**
Don. 8/2—7/5/32.**G.**
Don. 9—25/5/35.**G.**
Don. 28/11—18/12/37.**G.**
Don. 10—22/6/40.**G.**
Don. 19/1—7/3/43.**G.**
Don. 3—22/9/45.**G.**
Don. 1/3—15/4/48.**G.**
Don. 16/11—8/12/50.**L/I.**
Don. 30/11—31/12/53.**G.**
Don. 17/4/57. *Not Repaired.*

BOILERS:
1244.
1647 *(new)* ?/11/05.
1249 *(ex1249)* ?/6/16.
7891 *(new)* 30/8/27.
7989 *(ex4055)* 25/5/35.
9808 *(new)* 15/4/48.
9808 reno.21626 8/12/50.

SHED:
Doncaster.

RENUMBERED:
4244 1/11/24.
8843 1/12/46.
68843 15/4/48.

CONDEMNED: 22/4/57.
Cut up at Doncaster.

The engines in the batches which became Nos.4216 to 4290 had 3ft 3in. built-up chimneys from new.

A later version of the built-up chimney was similar but 2in. taller at 3ft 5in.

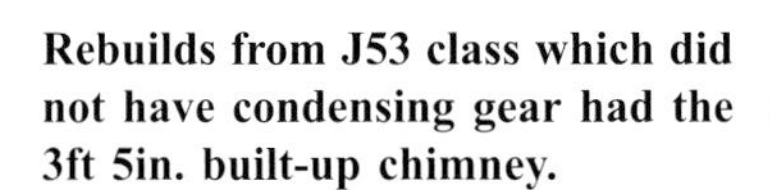

Rebuilds from J53 class which did not have condensing gear had the 3ft 5in. built-up chimney.

Condenser-fitted rebuilds had a built-up chimney but only 2ft 11$^{1}/_{2}$in. tall.

Although the 2ft 11½in. chimney kept the height within the Metropolitan load gauge, starting 22nd December 1931 with No.3975, a 2ft 10in. chimney was fitted and became standard for the condensing type engines in the class.

During the war, Stratford took on maintenance of some of the class, and due to a shortage of castings, some J52's had to make do with a stovepipe chimney. Out 5th May 1945, No.4233 (8832 later) was the first, followed by No.4290 on the 31st of that month. In 1946 Nos.8771 (26th March) and 8874 (14th September) were also fitted. These chimneys were neatly made by welding to an existing base and cowl.

This stovepipe survived two General repairs at Stratford, on 26th June 1948, and (as shown here) on 24th February 1951. No.68832 took this chimney to Doncaster on 5th January 1954.

No.68832's final repair was at Doncaster works and when out 28th January 1954, its stovepipe chimney had been replaced by a 2ft 11½in. standard cast chimney.

4245

Sharp Stewart & Co. 4490.

To Traffic 5/1899.

REPAIRS:
Don. 29/4--26/6/20.**G**.
Don. 19/7—8/11/24.**G**.
Don. 12/12/27—18/2/28.**G**.
Don. 15/2—23/3/30.**G**.
Don. 8/10—17/12/32.**G**.
Don. 18/10—9/11/35.**G**.
Don. 8/5—4/6/38.**G**.
Don. 26/10—23/11/40.**G**.
Don. 21/10—20/11/43.**G**.
Don. 10/2—16/3/46.**G**.
Don. 2/11—10/12/48.**G**.
Don. 4/2/51—9/1/52.**H/I**.
WM4 bronze axle-boxes fitted.
Don. 8/10/54. *Not Repaired.*

BOILERS:
1245.
1240 *(ex1240)* 26/6/20.
7987 *(new)* 18/2/28.
7891 *(ex4244)* 9/11/35.
7892 *(ex4247)* 4/6/38.
9503 *(new)* 16/3/46.
9816 *(new)* 10/12/48.
9816 reno.21640 9/1/52.

SHEDS:
Doncaster.
New England 19/1/50.

RENUMBERED:
4245 8/11/24.
8844 1/12/46.
68844 10/12/48.

CONDEMNED: 25/10/54.
Cut up at Doncaster.

4246

Sharp Stewart & Co. 4491.

To Traffic 5/1899.

REPAIRS:
Don. ?/?—?/11/07.**G**.
Don. 10/1—11/3/22.**G**.
Don. 2/6—8/11/24.**G**.
Don. 14/9—5/11/27.**G**.
Don. 2/1—7/2/30.**G**.
Don. 15/2—7/5/32.**G**.
Don. 9—26/1/35.**G**.
Don. 23/9—16/10/37.**G**.
Don. 26/12/39—17/2/40.**G**.
Don. 17/10—15/11/42.**G**.
Don. 26/3—28/4/45.**G**.
Don. 29/9—24/10/47.**G**.
Don. 10/5/50. *Not Repaired.*
To Service Stock 29/5/50.
Don. 21—25/6/54.**N/C**.

BOILERS:
1246.
1248 *(ex1248)* ?/11/07.
6992 *(ex E1 994)* 8/11/24.
6879 *(ex4049)* 7/2/30.
8746 *(new)* 26/1/35.
8491 *(ex4210)* 16/10/37.
8439 *(ex8870)* 24/10/47.
8439 reno.S.B.924 29/5/50.

SHEDS:
Doncaster.
Doncaster Works 27/5/50.

RENUMBERED:
4246 8/11/24.
8845 6/10/46.
68845 10/6/50.
DEPT'L No. 1 26/11/52.

WITHDRAWN: 29/5/50.
CONDEMNED: 17/2/58.
Cut up at Doncaster.

4247

Sharp Stewart & Co. 4492.

To Traffic 5/1899.

REPAIRS:
Don. ?/?—?/7/06.**G**.
Don. 4/6—17/9/21.**G**.
Don. 19/6—6/9/24.**G**.
Don. 30/9/26—25/2/27.**G**.
Don. 8/2—8/3/30.**G**.
Don. 27/2—19/3/32.**G**.
Don. 13—27/10/34.**G**.
Don. 26/6—3/7/37.**L**.
Don. 12—19/2/38.**G**.
Don. 26/4—24/5/41.**G**.
Don. 19/2—4/3/44.**G**.
Don. 26/10—9/11/46.**G**.
Don. 7—28/12/48.**G**.
Don. 18/2—14/3/52.**G**.
Don. 13/12/54—11/1/55.**G**.

BOILERS:
1247.
1266 *(ex1266)* ?/7/06.
7886 *(new)* 25/2/27.
7892 *(ex4223)* 27/10/34.
8433 *(ex4205)* 19/2/38.
8437 *(ex8882)* 9/11/46.
10511 *(new)* 28/12/48.
21644 14/3/52.
21777 *(ex68791)* 11/1/55.

SHEDS:
Doncaster.
New England 19/1/50.
Hornsey 4/3/56.
King's Cross 22/2/59.

RENUMBERED:
4247 6/9/24.
8846 15/12/46.
68846 28/12/48.

SOLD: 8/5/59. *For private preservation by W.G. Smith of John Mowlem & Son.*

4248

Sharp Stewart & Co. 4493.

To Traffic 5/1899.

REPAIRS:
Don. ?/?—?/1/07.**G**.
Don. 26/2—29/5/20.**G**.
Don. 5/12/24—4/4/25.**G**.
Don. 19/12/27—25/2/28.**G**.
Don. 17/2—29/3/30.**G**.
Don. 30/7—15/10/32.**G**.
Don. 7—28/9/35.**G**.
Don. 13/2—5/3/38.**G**.
Don. 30/7—24/8/40.**G**.
Don. 16/4—30/5/43.**G**.
Don. 21/1—23/2/46.**G**.
Don. 9/4—14/5/48.**G**.
Don. 31/1—22/2/51.**G**.
Don. 1—30/6/54.**G**.
Don. 3—6/7/54.**N/C**.
Don. 1/8/58. *Not Repaired.*

BOILERS:
1248.
1644 *(new)* ?/1/07.
8650 *(new)* 15/10/32.
8321 *(ex4258)* 5/3/38.
8473 *(ex3964)* 24/8/40.
8259 *(ex4270)* 30/5/43.
8322 *(ex8860)* 14/5/48.
21690 *(new)* 22/2/51.
21621 *(ex68800)* 30/6/54.

SHEDS:
Doncaster.
Mexborough 23/10/55.

RENUMBERED:
4248 4/4/25.
8847 10/11/46.
68847 14/5/48.

CONDEMNED: 1/8/58.
Cut up at Doncaster.

4249

Sharp Stewart & Co. 4494.

To Traffic 5/1899.

REPAIRS:
Don. ?/?—?/10/15.**G**.
Don. 8/2—3/5/19.**G**.
Don. 3/7—6/9/24.**G**.
Don. 19/11/27—28/1/28.**G**.
Don. 3/3—15/4/30.**G**.
Don. 6/7—15/10/32.**G**.
Don. 2/10—2/11/35.**G**.
Don. 29/5—25/6/38.**G**.
Don. 15/11—14/12/40.**G**.
Don. 27/8—18/9/43.**G**.
Don. 30/9—27/10/45.**G**.
Don. 5/7—5/8/49.**G**.
Don. 4—7/2/51.**N/C**.
Don. 25/11—19/12/51.**G**.
Don. 6—26/8/53.**C/L**.
Don. 28/2—24/3/55.**G**.
Don. 24/7/58. *Not Repaired.*

BOILERS:
1249.
1229 *(ex1241)* ?/10/15.
7985 *(new)* 28/1/28.
8351 *(ex4214)* 25/6/38.
8748 *(ex8837)* 5/8/49.
21639 19/12/51.
21728 *(ex68799)* 24/3/55.

SHEDS:
Doncaster.
Ardsley 22/10/44.
Bradford 13/1/45.
Ardsley 21/1/45.

RENUMBERED:
4249 6/9/24.
8848 29/9/46.
68848 5/8/49.

CONDEMNED: 24/7/58.
Cut up at Doncaster.

4250

Sharp Stewart & Co. 4495.

To Traffic 5/1899.

REPAIRS:
Don. ?/?—?/5/12.**G**.
Don. 31/10/19—31/1/20.**G**.
Don. 31/1—9/6/23.**G**.
Don. 3/6—22/8/25.**G**.
Don. 23/3—17/11/28.**G**.
Don. 20/12/30—12/1/31.**G**.
Don. 4/3—3/6/33.**G**.
Don. 19/1—15/2/36.**G**.
Don. 17—29/8/38.**G**.

Ex Stratford on 18th May 1945, No.3979 also acquired a change of chimney to stovepipe, but also had a smokebox door on which GNR type destination board brackets were fitted. It kept these to withdrawal on 13th December 1954 as BR No.68781. As far as is known, no use in service was ever made of the brackets.

Ex Stratford 31st March 1951, No.68799 had a normal built-up chimney (*see* page 17, bottom). By early April 1954 the top part of the chimney had become a stovepipe by the welding on of a piece of steel tube. This must have been done by the workshop at King's Cross which was its only shed. Its next works visit proved to be its last because it was condemned at Doncaster on 4th October 1954. Of those which got a stovepipe, No.68799 was the only one without a beaded rim. King's Cross.

As No.4290, No.68889 had been fitted with a stovepipe chimney when ex Stratford on 31st May 1945, and this chimney survived another General repair ex Stratford 23rd November 1948.

No.68889 then only had one more works visit and on 6th October 1951 from a 'General' at Stratford it had reverted to a normal cast type chimney. King's Cross goods yard.

King's Cross engine No.68862 was ex Stratford works 24th September 1955 from a Non-Classified repair recorded as having been modified, and fitted with a short chimney for work on London Transport Executive lines.

4250 cont./
Don. 8/2—12/4/41.**G.**
Don. 14/12/43—22/1/44.**G.**
Don. 19/5—6/7/46.**G.**
Don. 2—25/7/48.**G.**
Don. 18/6—16/7/51.**G.**
Don. 2/9—5/10/54.**G.**
Don. 8—12/10/54.**N/C.**
Don. 26/11/57. *Not Repaired.*

BOILERS:
1250.
1264 *(ex1264 & spare)* ?/5/12.
8202 *(new)* 17/11/28.
8214 *(ex4280)* 15/2/36.
8439 *(ex4243)* 29/8/38.
8202 *(ex3977)* 22/1/44.
8751 *(ex3965)* 6/7/46.
9809 *(new)* 25/7/48.
21696 *(new)* 16/7/51.
21681 5/10/54.

SHED:
Doncaster.

RENUMBERED:
4250 22/8/25.
8849 12/12/46.
68849 24/7/48.

CONDEMNED: 16/12/57.
Cut up at Doncaster.

4251

Doncaster 944.

To Traffic 12/1901.

REPAIRS:
Don. 4/9—16/12/22.**G.**
Don. 29/6—17/10/25.**G.**
Don. 28/12/28—16/2/29.**G.**
Don. 9/2—5/3/32.**G.**
Don. 15/8—21/9/35.**G.**
Don. 16/10—17/12/39.**G.**
Don. 15/7—21/8/43.**G.**
Don. 14/7—7/9/46.**G.**
Don. 22/1—11/2/49.**G.**
Don. 14/6—24/7/50.**C/L.**
Don. 13/1—7/2/52.**G.**
WM4 bronze axle-boxes fitted.
Don. 12/10/54. *Not Repaired.*

BOILERS:
1251.
1468 *(exE1 868)* 17/10/25.
8499 *(new)* 5/3/32.
8426 *(ex8775)* 11/2/49.
21641 7/2/52.

SHEDS:
Hornsey.
New England 26/2/42.

RENUMBERED:
4251 17/10/25.
8850 23/9/46.
68850 11/2/49.

CONDEMNED: 25/10/54.
Cut up at Doncaster.

4252

Doncaster 945.

To Traffic 12/1901.

REPAIRS:
Don. 16/3—14/5/21.**G.**
Don. 8/12/23—15/3/24.**G.**
Don. 29/4—15/7/27.**G.**
Don. 8/2—7/6/30.**G.**
Don. 2/3—5/5/34.**G.**
Don. 5—21/8/37.**G.**
Don. 23/11—28/12/40.**G.**
Str. 3/10—3/11/45.**G.**
Str. 4/10—26/11/49.**G.**
Don. 10/12/53—16/1/54.**G.**
Don. 1/5/57. *Not Repaired.*

BOILERS:
1252.
6941 *(ex1287)* 14/5/21.
1159 *(exJ4 1143)* 15/3/24.
8424 *(new)* 7/6/30.
8480 *(ex4273)* 21/8/37.
7894 *(ex4227)* 3/11/45.
9641 *(new)* 26/11/49.
21678 16/1/54

SHEDS:
Hornsey.
Annesley 19/10/52.
Colwick 7/12/52.

RENUMBERED:
4252 15/3/24.
8851 10/8/46.
68851 26/11/49.

CONDEMNED: 6/5/57.
Cut up at Doncaster.

4253

Doncaster 946.

To Traffic 12/1901.

REPAIRS:
Don. ?/?—?/1/16.**G.**
Don. 2/11/21—2/1/22.**G.**
Don. 15/12/24—7/3/25.**G.**
Don. 2/10/28—19/1/29.**G.**
Don. 5/1—14/3/31.**G.**
Don. 29/9—11/11/33.**G.**
Don. 13/4—16/5/36.**G.**
Don. 15/9—8/10/38.**G.**
Don. 19/5—23/6/41.**G.**
Don. 6—25/3/44.**G.**
Don. 16/6—22/7/47.**G.**
Don. 9/1—11/2/50.**G.**
Don. 1/2—3/3/53.**G.**

BOILERS:
1253.
1257 *(ex1257 & spare)* ?/1/16.
8213 *(new)* 19/1/29.
8211 *(ex4236)* 16/5/36.
8747 *(ex4276)* 23/6/41.
8341 *(ex68877)* 11/2/50.
21662 3/3/53.

SHEDS:
King's Cross.
Doncaster 17/3/23.
Boston 27/3/39.
New England 8/11/40.
Colwick 16/1/55.

RENUMBERED:
4253 7/3/25.
8852 7/10/46.
68852 11/2/50.

CONDEMNED: 31/12/55.
Into Don. for cut up 31/12/55.

4254

Doncaster 947.

To Traffic 12/1901.

REPAIRS:
Don. ?/?—?/8/09.**G.**
Don. ?/?—?/6/12.**G.**
Don. 15/6—7/8/20.**G.**
Don. 8/1—21/4/23.**G.**
Don. 27/2—3/7/26.**G.**
Don. 16/3—11/5/29.**G.**
Don. 5/4—23/7/32.**G.**
Don. 1/3—4/4/36.**G.**
Don. 3/11—30/12/39.**G.**
Don. 20/6—15/7/44.**G.**
Don. 21/7—7/9/48.**G.**
Don. 30/1—23/2/52.**C/L.**
Don. 9/3—1/4/53.**G.**

BOILERS:
1254.
1258 *(ex1258)* ?/8/09.
1255 *(ex1255 & spare)* ?/6/12.
1679 *(ex1273)* 21/4/23.
8519 *(new)* 23/7/32.
9156 *(new)* 30/12/39.
8658 *(ex8799)* 7/9/48.
8658 reno.21747 23/2/52.
21620 *(ex68810)* 1/4/53.

SHEDS:
Hornsey.
Doncaster 19/10/52.

RENUMBERED:
4254 *at shed 2/25.*
8853 8/12/46.
68853 7/9/48.

CONDEMNED: 12/7/56.
Into Don. for cut up 12/7/56.

4255

Doncaster 948.

To Traffic 12/1901.

REPAIRS:
Don. ?/?—?/5/10.**G.**
Don. 11/3—8/5/20.**G.**
Don. 29/10/24—31/1/25.**G.**
Don. 27/5—10/8/27.**G.**
Don. 19/4—12/6/30.**G.**
Don. 17/9—8/10/32.**G.**
Don. 8/3—6/4/35.**G.**
Don. 20/10—13/11/37.**G.**
Don. 15/7—17/8/40.**G.**
Don. 13/3—15/4/44.**G.**
Don. 31/12/44—10/2/45.**H.**
Str. 29/1—11/5/48.**G.**
Str. 8/5—29/6/51.**G.**
Don. 14/7/54. *Not Repaired.*

BOILERS:
1255.
1254 *(ex1254)* ?/5/10.
7888 *(new)* 10/8/27.
7900 *(ex4275)* 13/11/37.
8207 *(ex8855)* 11/5/48.
21735 29/6/51.

SHED:
King's Cross.

RENUMBERED:
4255 31/1/25.
8854 23/11/46.
68854 11/5/48.

CONDEMNED: 19/7/54.
Cut up at Doncaster.

4256

Doncaster 949.

To Traffic 12/1901.

REPAIRS:
Don. ?/?—?/5/16.**G.**
Don. 4/5—30/7/21.**G.**
Don. 11/2—4/4/25.**G.**

Although height restriction was not concerned, in the fifties at least five, Nos.68758, 68828, 68858 (Departmental No.2), 68873 and 68877 were fitted with a 2ft 5in. chimney taken from withdrawn C12 class engines.

All the class had continuous boiler handrails arched over the smokebox door, and with a lamp bracket above it, fixed on the front plate of the smokebox. Whilst No.68777 had both these details, when ex Stratford 7th August 1948 its smokebox door also carried a short cross rail and another lamp iron.

Even on engines rebuilt from J53 the early Stirling type safety valves in a brass trumpet were still used, No.922N being a J52 from 12th January 1924.

The shorter, wider brass cover for the safety valves also continued in use on rebuilds, No.4051 having one to July 1926.

4256 cont./
Don. 18/9—20/12/28.**G**.
Don. 7/3—11/6/32.**G**.
Don. 27/9—2/11/35.**G**.
Don. 12/7—24/8/40.**G**.
Don. 27/8—16/9/44.**G**.
Don. 1/1—8/3/48.**G**.
Str. 12/9—21/10/50.**G**.
Don. 4—28/5/53.**G**.

BOILERS:
1256.
1228 *(ex1203)* ?/5/16.
8207 *(new)* 20/12/28.
8492 *(ex8828)* 8/3/48.
21721 21/10/50.
21671 28/5/53.

SHEDS:
Hornsey.
King's Cross 8/10/38.
Hornsey 24/8/39.
King's Cross 14/9/42.
Hatfield 25/11/45.
King's Cross 13/1/46.

RENUMBERED:
4256 4/4/25.
8855 23/11/46.
E8855 8/3/48.
68855 21/10/50.

CONDEMNED: 14/11/56.
Into Don. for cut up 14/11/56.

4257

Doncaster 950.

To Traffic 12/1901.

REPAIRS:
Don. ?/?—?/12/12.**G**.
Don. 10/4—12/6/20.**G**.
Don. 16/6—11/10/24.**G**.
Don. 12/11/27—21/1/28.**G**.
Don. 20/4—11/7/31.**G**.
Don. 11/1—2/2/35.**G**.
Don. 21/4—14/5/38.**G**.
Don. 19/12/42—7/3/43.**G**.
Don. 13/7—2/10/47.**G**.
Str. 10/9—19/10/51.**G**.

BOILERS:
1257.
1258 *(ex1254)* ?/12/12.
7988 *(new)* 21/1/28.
8345 *(ex4289)* 14/5/38.
8209 *(ex8878)* 2/10/47.
21740 19/10/51.

SHEDS:
Hornsey.
Doncaster 19/10/52.

RENUMBERED:
4257 11/10/24.
8856 10/8/46.
68856 19/10/51.

CONDEMNED: 23/11/55.
Into Don. for cut up 23/11/55.

4258

Doncaster 951.

To Traffic 12/1901.

REPAIRS:
Don. ?/?—?/10/08.**G**.
Don. 19/8—26/10/18.**G**.
Don. 29/2—7/6/24.**G**.
Don. 1/12/26—16/2/27.**G**.
Don. 21/12/29—11/1/30.**G**.
Don. 12/12/31—20/2/32.**G**.
Hunt & Mitton lubrication to axleboxes fitted.
Don. 22/2—16/3/35.**G**.
Don. 28/10—20/11/37.**G**.
Don. 4/2—23/3/40.**G**.
Don. 8/5—5/6/43.**G**.
Don. 7/10—10/11/45.**G**.
Don. 29/9—24/10/47.**G**.
Don. 2—27/12/50.**H/I**.
Don. 27/2—9/3/51.**C/L**.
Don. 6—30/4/54.**G**.
Don. 14/4/58. *Not Repaired.*

BOILERS:
1258.
1203 *(ex1203)* ?/10/08.
1643 *(ex1242)* 26/10/18.
8321 *(new)* 11/1/30.
7983 *(ex4240)* 20/11/37.
7901 *(ex8765)* 24/10/47.
7901 reno.21627 27/12/50.
21699 *(ex68887)* 30/4/54.

SHEDS:
Doncaster.
Ardsley 23/11/52.

RENUMBERED:
4258 7/6/24.
8857 28/4/46.
68857 27/12/50.

CONDEMNED: 14/4/58.
Cut up at Doncaster.

4259

Doncaster 952.

To Traffic 12/1901.

REPAIRS:
Don. ?/?—?/5/13.**G**.
Don. 30/3—9/7/21.**G**.
Don. 29/6—5/9/25.**G**.
Don. 22/9—21/12/28.**G**.
Don. 15/8—3/10/31.**G**.
Don. 30/6—25/8/34.**G**.
Don. 11/11—12/12/36.**G**.
Don. 16/2—8/4/39.**G**.
Don. 27/9—15/11/41.**G**.
Don. 29/12/43—22/1/44.**G**.
Don. 11/7—17/8/46.**G**.
Don. 26/5—25/6/48.**G**.
Don. 22/8—23/9/52.**G**.
To Service Stock 11/3/56.

BOILERS:
1259.
1202 *(ex1202)* ?/5/13.
1245 *(ex1245)* 9/7/21.
8209 *(new)* 21/12/28.
8478 *(ex4262)* 12/12/36.
8255 *(ex4268)* 8/4/39.
8215 *(ex3965)* 22/1/44.
9813 *(new)* 25/6/48.
21652 23/9/52.
21698 (ex68842) reno.S.B.1079 11/3/56.

SHEDS:
Colwick.
Doncaster 18/12/49.
Doncaster Works 11/3/56.

RENUMBERED:
4259 5/9/25.
8858 14/7/46.
68858 25/6/48.
DEPT'L No. 2 11/3/56.

WITHDRAWN: 16/12/55.
CONDEMNED: 3/2/61.
Into Don. for cut up 3/2/61.

(above) **On engines built as J52 the Ramsbottom safety valves had Ivatt's design of cast iron casing - *see* page 51, top, where No.4231 had Ramsbottom valves without a casing on a boiler which started work in September 1908 and was in regular use until October 1948.**

Starting from October 1926 replacement boilers had Ross 'pop' safety valves which the whole class duly acquired.

(below) **On some of the 1923/24 rebuilds the whistle was placed on top of the cab.**

Standard whistle position was on the front plate of the cab, and those which had whistles on top of the cab (*see* page 47, bottom) soon had it moved lower down.

The usual position for the LNER number plate was on the bunker but some had it on the cab side.

On the first thirty Class J53 (Nos.3921 to 3930 and 3961 to 3980) the vertical handrails to the cab were of different length and they remained so when rebuilt to J52 and to withdrawal - *see* page 43, top.

4260

Doncaster 953.

To Traffic 2/1902.

REPAIRS:
Don. ?/?—?/5/13.**G.**
Don. ?/?—9/4/21.**L.**
Scarab oil burning system fitted.
Don. 1/2—1/4/22.**G.**
Oil firing removed.
Don. 30/1—14/6/24.**G.**
Don. 14/4—27/6/27.**G.**
Don. 22/8—11/10/30.**G.**
Don. 3/7—9/9/33.**G.**
Don. 23/11—7/12/35.**G.**
Don. 15/10—21/11/36.**L.**
Don. 19/5—13/6/38.**G.**
Don. 23/2—29/4/39.**L.**
Don. 15/2—8/3/41.**G.**
Don. 18/10—13/11/43.**G.**
Don. 27/4—2/6/45.**G.**
Don. 14/3—27/4/47.**G.**
Don. 19/6—22/7/49.**G.**
Don. 31/10—29/11/51.**G.**
Don. 12/7/54. *Not Repaired.*

BOILERS:
1260.
1250 *(ex1250)* ?/5/13.
1132 *(exJ4 329)* 14/6/24.
7889 *(new)* 27/6/27.
8749 *(new)* 7/12/35.
8436 *(ex4281)* 13/6/38.
8352 *(ex4231)* 13/11/43.
8214 *(ex8792)* 27/4/47.
8479 *(ex8886)* 22/7/49.
21637 29/11/51.

SHEDS:
Colwick.
Ardsley 13/6/38.
Colwick 27/7/38.

RENUMBERED:
4260 14/6/24.
8859 6/10/46.
68859 22/7/49.

CONDEMNED: 2/8/54.
Cut up at Doncaster.

4261

Doncaster 954.

To Traffic 12/1901.

REPAIRS:
Don. ?/?—?/7/13.**G.**
Don. ?/?—?/7/17.**G.**
Don. 13/9/20—8/1/21.**G.**
Don. 15/12/24—14/3/25.**G.**
Don. 27/6—15/9/27.**G.**
Don. 14/12/29—31/1/30.**G.**
Don. 23/1—7/5/32.**G.**
Don. 8/2—2/3/35.**G.**
Don. 1—20/8/38.**G.**
Don. 21/4—17/5/41.**G.**
Don. 13/12/43—8/1/44.**G.**
Don. 20/8—5/10/46.**G.**
Don. 1—8/5/47.**L.**
Don. 7—31/12/47.**H.**
Don. 23/5—18/6/49.**G.**
Don. 24/11—23/12/53.**G.**
Don. 17/12/57. *Not Repaired.*

BOILERS:
1261.
1262 *(ex1262)* ?/7/13.
1647 *(ex1244)* ?/7/17.
8322 *(new)* 31/1/30.
9807 *(new)* 31/12/47.
9807 reno.21677 23/12/53.

SHEDS:
King's Cross.
New England 11/4/35.
Doncaster 13/2/44.
Colwick 30/10/55.

RENUMBERED:
4261 14/3/25.
8860 7/7/46.
68860 18/6/49.

CONDEMNED: 23/12/57.
Cut up at Doncaster.

4262

Doncaster 955.

To Traffic 2/1902.

REPAIRS:
Don. ?/?—?/2/13.**G.**
Don. 23/9—6/11/20.**G.**
Don. 26/11/24—17/7/25.**G.**
Don. 14/7—1/9/28.**G.**
Don. 24/1—11/4/31.**G.**
Don. 15/1—31/3/34.**G.**
Don. 12/10—7/11/36.**G.**
Don. 12—19/11/36.**N/C.**
Don. 24/10—23/12/39.**G.**
Don. 22/11/43—8/1/44.**G.**
Don. 27/11/46—18/1/47.**G.**
Str. 3/10—12/11/49.**G.**
Str. 2/7—22/8/52.**G.**

BOILERS:
1262.
1207 *(ex1235 & spare)* ?/2/13.
7040 *(exE1 3814)* 17/7/25.
8478 *(new)* 11/4/31.
8262 *(ex4284)* 7/11/36.
8746 *(ex3374)* 18/1/47.
9640 *(new)* 12/11/49.
21750 22/8/52.

SHEDS:
King's Cross.
New England 10/4/31.
King's Cross 15/4/35.

RENUMBERED:
4262 17/7/25.
8861 27/11/46.
68861 12/11/49.

CONDEMNED: 10/10/55.
Into Don. for cut up 10/10/55.

4263

Doncaster 956.

To Traffic 2/1902.

REPAIRS:
Don. ?/?—?/12/14.**G.**
Don. 16/8—25/11/22.**G.**
Don. 9/11/25—6/2/26.**G.**
Don. 17/9—7/12/28.**G.**
Don. 4/10—22/11/30.**G.**
Don. 12/11/32—21/1/33.**G.**
Don. 27/9—26/10/35.**G.**
Don. 17/3—9/4/38.**G.**
Don. 7/12/40—3/1/41.**G.**
Don. 1—23/9/44.**G.**
Don. 8—18/11/44.**L.**
Str. 5/4—26/6/48.**G.**
Str. 18/8—3/9/48.**L.**
Str. 30/5—21/7/51.**G.**
Don. 16/6—22/7/54.**G.**
Don. 26—29/7/54.**N/C.**
Str. 24/8—24/9/55.**N/C.**
Don. 13/10/58. *Not Repaired.*

BOILERS:
1263.
1243 *(ex1207)* ?/12/14.
8206 *(new)* 7/12/28.
9639 *(new)* 26/6/48.
21736 21/7/51.
21690 *(ex68847)* 22/7/54.

SHEDS:
Trafford Park.
Gorton 25/4/25.
King's Cross 21/2/26.
Doncaster 31/8/58.

RENUMBERED:
4263 6/2/26.
8862 28/11/46.
68862 26/6/48.

CONDEMNED: 13/10/58.
Cut up at Doncaster.

4264

Doncaster 957.

To Traffic 3/1902.

REPAIRS:
Don. ?/?—?/6/09.**G.**
Don. 27/9—6/12/19.**G.**
Don. 17/4—27/9/24.**G.**
Don. 17/9—12/11/27.**G.**
Don. 27/1—31/5/30.**G.**
Don. 19/12/33—10/3/34.**G.**
Don. 18/6—11/7/36.**G.**
Don. 1/4—3/6/39.**G.**
Don. 17/11—20/12/41.**G.**
Don. 10/3—8/4/44.**G.**
Don. 24/1—8/3/47.**G.**
Don. 23/5—16/6/49.**G.**
Don. 28/2—21/3/52.**G.**
Don. 21/2—16/3/55.**G.**
Don. 8/5/58. *Not Repaired.*

BOILERS:
1264.
1238 *(ex1238)* ?/6/09.
1653 *(ex J4 345)* 27/9/24.
8422 *(new)* 31/5/30.
8751 *(new)* 11/7/36.
7897 *(ex4210)* 20/12/41.
8472 *(ex3973)* 8/3/47.
21645 21/3/52.
21642 *(ex68869)* 16/3/55.

SHEDS:
Doncaster.
Colwick 31/5/30.

RENUMBERED:
4264 27/9/24.
8863 1/12/46.
68863 16/6/49.

CONDEMNED: 8/5/58.
Cut up at Doncaster.

4265

Doncaster 958.

To Traffic 3/1902.

REPAIRS:
Don. 22/9—11/11/22.**G.**
Don. 9/2—25/4/25.**G.**
Don. 19/2—23/4/27.**G.**
Don. 28/6—16/8/30.**G.**
Don. 1/10—3/12/32.**G.**
Don. 13/6—13/7/35.**G.**
Don. 27/1—26/2/38.**G.**
Don. 28/10—30/11/40.**G.**
Don. 22/7—12/8/44.**G.**
Str. 28/5—3/9/47.**G.**
Str. 23/5—1/7/50.**G.**

Beginning on Neilson built No.4046 these cab handrails were made the same height as they were on all subsequent engines.

On the first fifty, to No.4215 built in June 1897, the sandboxes were of rectangular shape and sanding was by gravity.

Starting in August 1897 on Nos.111 and 155, Doncaster changed to a hopper type sandbox at the front end, and this was used from then on.

As shown in the illustrations on pages 13, top, and 25, top, front end sand delivery was appreciably ahead of where it was needed, and from about 1925, the pipes were lengthened and curved around the brake hanger. On 8th March 1932 No.3975 working near Denmark Hill on the Southern Railway had a sandpipe broken off during a brake application, this fell onto the live rail and caused a short circuit, as a result of which alteration had to be made.

From 1932 the sandpipe arrangement at the front thus reverted to what it had been pre-1925.

To No.4215 the brake pull rods were outside the wheels and remained this way.

For the last two built as J53 and all those as J52, the brake pull rod was between the wheels.

Normal lubrication for cylinders and valves was a pair of displacement type fitted in the waist of the smokebox on each side.

Ex Doncaster works on 20th February 1932, No.4258 was fitted with a Hunt & Mitton automatic lubricator to serve the axleboxes. No others were so fitted and the Hunt & Mitton appliance was taken off, probably at the March 1935 repair.

The Hunt & Mitton lubricator was mounted on the left hand running plate and driven from the motion between the frames.

4265 cont./
Don. 23/1—16/2/53.**G**.

BOILERS:
1265.
7890 *(new)* 23/4/27.
7984 *(ex4279)* 26/2/38.
8655 *(ex8881)* 3/9/47.
8204 *(ex8834)* 1/7/50.
21661 16/2/53.

SHEDS:
Trafford Park.
Bidston 20/6/29.
New England 6/8/30.
King's Cross 8/1/31.

RENUMBERED:
4265 25/4/25.
8864 23/11/46.
68864 1/7/50.

CONDEMNED: 19/10/55.
Into Don. for cut up 19/10/55.

4266

Doncaster 959.

To Traffic 3/1902.

REPAIRS:
Don. ?/?—?/12/14.**G**.
Don. 5/1—16/3/18.**G**.
Don. 25/7—20/10/23.**G**.
Don. 4/1—6/3/26.**G**.
Don. 24/12/28—22/6/29.**G**.
Don. 13/9—21/11/31.**G**.
Don. 9—26/1/35.**G**.
Don. 26/9—16/10/37.**G**.
Don. 29/10—9/12/39.**G**.
Don. 14/9—11/10/42.**G**.
Don. 7/8—8/9/45.**G**.
Don. 20/2—19/3/48.**G**.
Don. 26/9—17/10/51.**G**.
Don. 27/10/55. *Not Repaired.*

BOILERS:
1266.
1239 *(ex1204)* ?/12/14.
8261 *(new)* 22/6/29.
8424 *(ex4252)* 16/10/37.
8432 *(ex4053)* 8/9/45.
8498 *(ex8807)* 19/3/48.
21633 17/10/51.

SHED:
Doncaster.

RENUMBERED:
1266N 20/10/23.
4266 6/3/26.
8865 16/11/46.
68865 19/3/48.

CONDEMNED: 27/10/55.
Cut up at Doncaster.

4267

Doncaster 960.

To Traffic 3/1902.

REPAIRS:
Don. 30/8—1/11/19.**G**.
Don. 5/4—6/8/23.**G**.
Don. 9/7—3/9/26.**G**.
Don. 1/9—28/12/29.**G**.
Don. 23/3—17/6/33.**G**.
Don. 6—28/12/35.**G**.
Don. 27/5—25/6/38.**G**.
Don. 24/10—23/11/40.**G**.
Don. 5/12/43—1/1/44.**G**.
Don. 13/12/46—1/2/47.**G**.
Don. 19/10—11/11/49.**G**.
Don. 6—29/1/53.**G**.
Don. 2/9/58. *Not Repaired.*

BOILERS:
1267.
8348 *(new)* 28/12/29.
7988 *(ex4257)* 25/6/38.
10514 *(new)* 11/11/49.
21659 29/1/53.

SHEDS:
New England.
Hornsey 6/9/53.

RENUMBERED:
4267 3/9/26.
8866 28/7/46.
68866 11/11/49.

CONDEMNED: 2/9/58.
Cut up at Doncaster.

4268

Doncaster 961.

To Traffic 4/1902.

REPAIRS:
Don. 20/1—13/3/20.**G**.
Don. 21/9—24/11/23.**G**.
Don. 9/7—3/9/26.**G**.
Don. 22/7—22/10/27.**G**.
Don. 11/9—25/10/30.**G**.
Don. 23/10—2/12/33.**G**.
Don. 15/2—7/3/36.**G**.
Don. 21/11—10/12/38.**G**.
Don. 23/4—31/5/41.**G**.
Don. 6/8—4/9/43.**G**.
Don. 18/12/45—2/2/46.**G**.
Str. 26/7—27/8/48.**G**.
Don. 19/2—14/3/51.**G**.
Don. 13/4—18/5/54.**G**.
Don. 15/1/58. *Not Repaired.*

BOILERS:
1268.
7896 *(new)* 22/10/27.
8255 *(ex4228)* 7/3/36.
7985 *(ex4249)* 10/12/38.
8426 *(ex3925 & spare)* 4/9/43.
8440 *(ex4271)* 2/2/46.
9812 *(new)* 27/8/48.
21692 *(new)* 14/3/51.

SHEDS:
New England.
Colwick 27/10/30.
Doncaster 18/12/49.
Hatfield 16/3/52.
King's Cross 3/1/54.
Hatfield 10/1/54.
King's Cross 27/6/54.
Hatfield 25/7/54.

RENUMBERED:
1268N 24/11/23.
4268 3/9/26.
8867 14/7/46.
68867 27/8/48.

CONDEMNED: 10/2/58.
Cut up at Doncaster.

4269

Doncaster 962.

To Traffic 3/1902.

REPAIRS:
Don. 10/5—2/9/22.**G**.
Don. 1/9—14/11/25.**G**.
Don. 26/10—9/11/29.**G**.
Don. 22/4—6/5/33.**G**.
Don. 25/4—16/5/36.**G**.
Don. 30/9—21/10/39.**G**.
Don. 25/4—9/5/42.**G**.
Don. 24/2—17/3/45.**G**.
Don. 28/10—3/12/47.**G**.
Don. 10/7—4/8/50.**G**.
Don. 12/4—5/5/53.**G**.
Don. 26/10/55. *Not Repaired.*

BOILERS:
1269.
8338 *(new)* 9/11/29.
10581 *(new)* 4/8/50.
21668 5/5/53.

SHEDS:
New England.
Ardsley 23/8/53.

RENUMBERED:
4269 14/11/25.
8868 28/7/46.
68868 4/8/50.

CONDEMNED: 28/10/55.
Cut up at Doncaster.

4270

Doncaster 963.

To Traffic 3/1902.

REPAIRS:
Don. 2/3—7/5/21.**G**.
Don. 2/9—20/12/24.**G**.
Don. 16/6—1/9/27.**G**.
Don. 14/2—29/3/30.**G**.
Don. 28/7—23/9/33.**G**.
Don. 15/6—11/7/36.**G**.
Don. 26/10—2/12/39.**G**.
Don. 16/3—17/4/43.**G**.
Don. 8/2—9/3/46.**G**.
Don. 30/9—5/11/48.**G**.
Don. 9/1—1/2/52.**H/I**.
Don. 22/12/54—22/1/55.**G**.
Don. 9/3/61. *Not Repaired.*

BOILERS:
1270.
7904 *(new)* 1/9/27.
8259 *(ex4290)* 11/7/36.
8340 *(ex4049 & sp.)* 17/4/43.
9501 *(new)* 9/3/46.
9501 reno.21642 1/2/52.
21638 *(ex68835)* 22/1/55.

SHEDS:
New England.
Doncaster 6/9/44.
Hornsey 31/8/58.
Ardsley 5/4/59.

RENUMBERED:
4270 20/12/24.
8869 6/10/46.
68869 5/11/48.

CONDEMNED: 20/3/61.
Cut up at Doncaster.

WORKS CODES:- Cow - Cowlairs. Dar - Darlington. Don - Doncaster. Ghd - Gateshead. Gor - Gorton. Inv - Inverurie. Kit - Kittybrewster. RSH - Robert, Stephenson & Hawthorn. Str - Stratford. Yk - York.
REPAIR CODES:- **C/H** - Casual Heavy. **C/L** - Casual Light. **G** - General. **H**- Heavy. **H/I** - Heavy Intermediate. **L** - Light. **L/I** - Light Intermediate. **N/C** - Non-Classified.

No.3924 was the first J52 to be withdrawn from traffic - on 9th March 1936. After standing at Doncaster works to 13th June 1936 (as seen here on 10th May 1936) it was transferred to Service Stock as an extra shunter at the works, but only until 14th September 1936 when it was condemned and broken up.

No.3964 had a similar experience to 3924. It was withdrawn from traffic on 15th August 1939 and although not transferred officially to Service Stock, Doncaster used it as a works shunter at least for the remainder of 1939 but it was cut up by July 1940 and its boiler went to No.4248.

A twenty-five year association of J52 class with Service Stock as Doncaster works shunters began when No.3980 moved from Running to Service stock on 9th November 1936. Recognition of its changed status showed by the use of $7^1/_2$in. instead of 12in. transfers for its number. This became 8782 on 14th November 1946 and 68782 on 3rd July 1948.

No.68782 was given a final General overhaul 30th June to 3rd July 1948, when it got its BRITISH RAILWAYS lettering and number. On 23rd June 1950 it was condemned and during July was cut up.

As a replacement for No.68782, No.68845 was transferred to Service Stock from 29th May 1950. It was overhauled, fitted with a smokebox number plate, and given its BR number from 10th June 1950. For more than four weeks it ran lettered as shown before this was painted out.

In August 1952, Service Stock engines were allocated a separate range of numbers from 1 to 100. No.68845 kept its smokebox number but on 26th November 1952 the bunker number was altered to No.1 DEPARTMENTAL LOCOMOTIVE. It retained that guise until condemned 17th February 1958.

LNER No.8816, shown here at Grantham in May 1950, was transferred from Running Stock on 29th May 1950 to become yard locomotive at Doncaster works. Ex General repair 21st May 1951, it changed to BR livery.

At the 21st May 1951 repair BR No.68816 was put on and a smokebox number plate was fitted. On 13th November 1952 the bunker designation was changed to No.2 DEPARTMENTAL LOCOMOTIVE, but it still kept the plate showing LNER 8816 on it. This engine was condemned on 11th March 1956 and then cut up, its identity as No.2 DEPARTMENTAL LOCOMOTIVE being taken on by No.68858 (*see* next).

No.68858 had been taken out of Running Stock on 16th December 1955 and condemned but was not broken up. Instead, on 11th March 1956 it became No.2 DEPARTMENTAL LOCOMOTIVE but lost its previous identity because both its oval and smokebox number plates were removed. It served to 3rd February 1961 when it was condemned and scrapped.

To replace No.1 DEPARTMENTAL LOCOMOTIVE in 1958, No.68840 was allocated. It had arrived in works on 9th January 1958 for normal repair so on 27th January it was transferred to Service Stock as No.9 DEPARTMENTAL LOCOMOTIVE. It kept its LNER 8840 oval plate on the cab side but lost the 68840 smokebox plate. It too was condemned on 3rd February 1961 and then scrapped, ending almost twenty-five years of J52 class in Service Stock.

4271

Doncaster 1087.

To Traffic 9/1905.

REPAIRS:
Don. 25/1—19/4/19.**G.**
Don. 17/4—9/7/23.**G.**
Don. 18/2—30/4/26.**G.**
Don. 26/7—6/12/29.**G.**
Don. 24/12/31—27/2/32.**G.**
Don. 8/10—10/11/34.**G.**
Don. 18/3—22/5/37.**G.**
Don. 2/8—30/9/39.**G.**
Don. 16/8—20/9/42.**G.**
Don. 17/1—17/2/45.**G.**
Don. 29/9—24/10/47.**G.**
Don. 22/1—12/2/51.**G.**
Don. 4/5—1/6/54.**H/I.**
Don. 20/1/58. *Not Repaired.*

BOILERS:
1678.
8344 *(new)* 6/12/29.
8440 *(ex3972)* 20/9/42.
8439 *(ex4250)* 17/2/45.
8491 *(ex8845)* 24/10/47.
21628 12/2/51.

SHEDS:
Doncaster.
Mexborough 23/10/55.

RENUMBERED:
4271 30/4/26.
8870 12/5/46.
68870 12/2/51.

CONDEMNED: 22/3/58.
Cut up at Doncaster.

4272

Doncaster 1088.

To Traffic 9/1905.

REPAIRS:
Don. ?/?—?/10/15.**G.**
Don. 13/9/21—16/1/22.**G.**
Don. 2/3—14/6/25.**G.**
Don. 27/9—1/11/28.**G.**
Don. 26/5—20/8/32.**G.**
Don. 20/7—15/8/36.**G.**
Don. 25/5—15/6/40.**G.**
Don. 13/12/43—1/1/44.**G.**
Don. 27/8—15/9/45.**G.**
Don. 23—28/9/45.**N/C.**
Don. 28/10—21/11/47.**G.**
Don. 11/4—9/5/51.**G.**
Don. 26/9—20/10/54.**G.**
Don. 21—23/10/54.**N/C.**
Don. 25/1/58. *Not Repaired.*

BOILERS:
1680.
1232 *(ex1238)* ?/10/15.
8199 *(new)* 1/11/28.
8352 *(ex8859)* 21/11/47.
21695 *(new)* 9/5/51.
21696 *(ex68849)* 20/10/54.

SHEDS:
Doncaster.
Mexborough 2/11/25.
Bradford 7/2/30.
Ardsley 16/5/38.
Colwick 18/12/55.

RENUMBERED:
4272 14/6/25.
8871 6/10/46.
68871 9/5/51.

CONDEMNED: 10/2/58.
Cut up at Doncaster.

4273

Doncaster 1089.

To Traffic 9/1905.

REPAIRS:
Don. 27/9/22—24/3/23.**G.**
Don. 20/12/27—25/2/28.**G.**
Don. 2/5—18/7/31.**G.**
Don. 1/8—1/9/34.**G.**
Don. 16/1—3/2/37.**G.**
Don. 20/3—22/4/40.**G.**
Don. 29/11—18/12/43.**G.**
Don. 17/11—14/12/46.**G.**
Don. 11—24/12/47.**L.**
Don. 3—20/8/48.**L.**
Don. 26/3—4/5/50.**G.**
Don. 17—21/3/51.**N/C.**
Don. 13/10—5/11/52.**G.**
Don. 16/8/56. *Not Repaired.*

BOILERS:
1679.
6880 24/3/23.
1246 *(ex4227)* 25/2/28.
8480 *(new)* 18/7/31.
7986 *(ex3924)* 3/2/37.
8323 *(ex8876)* 4/5/50.
21654 5/11/52.

SHEDS:
Trafford Park.
Gorton 13/5/25.
Trafford Park ?/?/?.
Bidston 5/11/29.
Colwick 22/4/30.
Ardsley 3/8/38.

RENUMBERED:
4273 *after* 12/24.
8872 7/7/46.
68872 20/8/48.

CONDEMNED: 21/8/56.
Cut up at Doncaster.

4274

Doncaster 1090.

To Traffic 10/1905.

REPAIRS:
Don. 6/1—10/5/22.**G.**
Don. 22/1—28/3/25.**G.**
Don. 3/7—24/8/28.**G.**
Don. 23/2—16/5/31.**G.**
Don. 22/9—11/11/33.**G.**
Don. 28/7—4/9/36.**G.**
Don. 31/7—8/11/39.**G.**
Don. 3/6—24/7/43.**G.**
Str. 9/12/45—5/1/46.**G.**
Str. 7/10—16/11/48.**G.**
Str. 20/9—28/10/49.**C/L.**
Str. 6/2—15/3/52.**G.**

BOILERS:
1681.
25 *(exE1 760)* 10/5/22.
7981 *(ex4208)* 16/5/31.
9497 *(new)* 5/1/46.
8497 *(ex8777)* 16/11/48.
21748 15/3/52.

SHEDS:
Trafford Park.
King's Cross 19/9/28.
Hornsey 25/11/51.
Colwick 13/7/52.

RENUMBERED:
4274 28/3/25.
8873 6/12/46.
68873 16/11/48.

CONDEMNED: 30/9/55.
Into Don. for cut up 30/9/55.

4275

Doncaster 1091.

To Traffic 10/1905.

REPAIRS:
Don. 11/6—7/8/20.**G.**
Don. 16/6—6/9/24.**G.**
Don. 27/5—29/7/27.**G.**
Don. 1/2—22/3/30.**G.**
Don. 2/4—16/7/32.**G.**
Don. 2/3—6/4/35.**G.**
Don. 3—23/10/37.**G.**
Don. 13—30/6/40.**G.**
Don. 31/10—7/12/43.**G.**
Str. 9/8—14/9/46.**G.**
Str. 14/2—13/5/50.**G.**
Don. 10/4—5/5/53.**G.**
Don. 16/10/57. *Not Repaired.*

BOILERS:
1682.
7900 *(new)* 29/7/27.
8746 *(ex4246)* 23/10/37.
8518 *(ex3969)* 14/9/46.
8657 *(ex68826)* 13/5/50.
8657 reno.21669 5/5/53.

SHED:
King's Cross.

RENUMBERED:
4275 6/9/24.
8874 27/7/46.
68874 13/5/50.

CONDEMNED: 16/10/57.
Cut up at Doncaster.

4276

Doncaster 1092.

To Traffic 10/1905.

REPAIRS:
Don. 6/1—25/5/22.**G.**
Don. 10/11/25—16/3/26.**G.**
Don. 4/8/28—26/1/29.**G.**
Don. 14/11/31—13/2/32.**G.**
Don. 31/12/34—26/1/35.**G.**
Don. 23/7—7/8/37.**G.**
Don. 12/3—20/4/40.**G.**
Don. 7/5—23/6/43.**G.**
Don. 31/1—9/3/46.**G.**
Don. 21/6—26/7/48.**G.**
Don. 12/3—11/4/51.**G.**
Don. 8—22/4/52.**N/C.**
Don. 29/4—26/5/54.**G.**
Don. 4/6/60. *Not Repaired.*

BOILERS:
1683.
384 16/3/26.
8215 *(new)* 26/1/29.
8747 *(new)* 26/1/35.
7898 *(ex4048)* 20/4/40.
9155 *(ex4210)* 9/3/46.
21630 11/4/51.
21632 26/5/54

SHEDS:
Lincoln.
Immingham *by* 5/24.
Lincoln 1/5/26.
Grantham 23/12/26.
Colwick 11/3/29.
Ardsley 7/12/52.

When the LNER took over, all J52 class were in unlined grey paint with numbers and letters in white shaded black. From 9th April 1921 to 1st February 1922 No.1260 was fitted for oil firing on the Scarab system with an 880 gallon oil tank in the bunker.

First LNER paintings changed the grey to black and added single red lining with the initials L&NER. The number was moved to the tank side and became 12in. instead of $7^{1}/_{2}$in. In the first half of 1923 thirteen of the class got the style depicted here: 1210 (24th March), 1273 (24th March), 1218 (31st March), 1277 (19th April), 1228 (21st April), 1254 (21st April), 1202 (5th May), 1204 (5th May), 1225 (22nd May), 1250 (9th June), 980 (12th June), 1217 (12th June) and 978 (20th June).

During the summer a slight change was made on the next three, the ampersand not being included. They were Nos.1271 (9th July), 921 (6th August) and 1267 (6th August).

For the next five months area suffix N, 4½in. high, was added to the number and thirteen acquired this style. In 1923: 1240N (1st September), 1050N, 1051N, 1242N, 1289N (all 8th September), 1266N (20th October), 1049N (2nd November), 1056N (17th November), 1268N (24th November), 926N (15th December), 972N (22nd December). In January 1924: 922N (12th), 929N (18th).

Starting with No.4203, ex works 9th February 1924, the full LNER number was used, and the red lining was applied to June 1928.

The painting economies decreed 31st May 1928, in Minute 841 of the Locomotive Committee led to only unlined black and one coat of varnish (instead of two) being put on thereafter.

4276 cont./
Colwick 18/12/55.
Hornsey 4/3/56.
Ardsley 8/2/59.

RENUMBERED:
4276 16/3/26.
8875 13/10/46.
68875 24/7/48.

CONDEMNED: 20/3/61.
Cut up at Doncaster.

4277

Doncaster 1093.

To Traffic 10/1905.

REPAIRS:
Don. 30/8—14/12/18.**G.**
Don. 18/1—19/4/23.**G.**
Don. 9/7—4/9/26.**G.**
Don. 17/12/29—1/2/30.**G.**
Don. 23/1—25/3/33.**G.**
Don. 19/12/35—11/1/36.**G.**
Don. 1/2—18/3/39.**G.**
Don. 29/12/41—18/1/42.**G.**
Don. 21/8—16/9/44.**G.**
Don. 4/5—20/6/47.**G.**
Don. 12/2—30/3/50.**G.**
Don. 12/1—3/2/53.**G.**
Don. 29/2/56. *Not Repaired.*

BOILERS:
1684.
8323 *(new)* 1/2/30.
8747 *(ex8852)* 30/3/50.
21660 3/2/53.

SHEDS:
New England.
Colwick 7/11/54.

RENUMBERED:
4277 31/1/25.
8876 6/10/46.
68876 30/3/50.

CONDEMNED: 5/3/56.
Cut up at Doncaster.

4278

Doncaster 1094.

To Traffic 11/1905.

REPAIRS:
Don. 13/1—6/5/22.**G.**
Don. 5/10—12/12/25.**G.**
Don. 23/5—24/11/28.**G.**
Don. 12/2—14/5/32.**G.**
Don. 16/11—1/12/34.**G.**
Don. 13—24/12/37.**G.**
Don. 19/8—5/10/40.**G.**
Don. 14/12/43—1/1/44.**G.**
Don. 30/12/46—8/2/47.**G.**
Don. 1—18/2/49.**C/L.**
Don. 3—27/1/50.**G.**
Don. 26/2—20/3/53.**G.**

BOILERS:
1685.
8203 *(new)* 24/11/28.
8341 *(ex4203)* 24/12/37.
8433 *(ex8765)* 27/1/50.
21665 20/3/53.

SHEDS:
New England.
Grantham 24/8/33.
Boston 14/3/34.
Grantham 23/3/34.
Colwick 8/4/56.

RENUMBERED:
4278 12/12/25.
8877 14/7/46.
68877 18/2/49.

CONDEMNED: 20/11/56.
Into Don. for cut up 20/11/56.

4279

Doncaster 1095.

To Traffic 11/1905.

REPAIRS:
Don. 7/5—19/6/20.**G.**
Don. 10/11/24—14/2/25.**G.**
Don. 6/11/27—7/1/28.**G.**
Don. 16/8—3/10/31.**G.**
Don. 29/7—1/9/34.**G.**
Don. 25/7—21/8/37.**G.**
Don. 4/7—17/8/40.**G.**
Don. 14/6—15/7/44.**G.**
Str. 30/5—18/8/47.**G.**
Str. 16/4—25/5/50.**G.**
Don. 27/4—20/5/53.**G.**

BOILERS:
1686.
7984 *(new)* 7/1/28.
8209 *(ex4259)* 21/8/37.
8744 *(ex4230)* 18/8/47.
8652 *(ex8772)* 25/5/50.
21670 20/5/53.

SHEDS:
New England.
King's Cross 11/4/35.

RENUMBERED:
4279 14/2/25.
8878 6/12/46.
68878 25/5/50.

CONDEMNED: 25/5/56.
Into Don. for cut up 25/5/56.

4280

Doncaster 1096.

To Traffic 11/1905.

REPAIRS:
Don. 12/6—31/7/20.**G.**
Don. 3/1—19/4/24.**G.**
Don. 5/8—30/10/26.**G.**
Don. 4/10/28—19/1/29.**G.**
Don. 12/11/32—14/1/33.**G.**
Don. 31/12/35—18/1/36.**G.**
Don. 21/4—1/7/39.**G.**
Don. 3/1—27/2/43.**G.**
Don. 30/9—2/11/46.**G.**
Don. 17/3—19/4/48.**L.**
Don. 2—21/10/49.**G.**
Don. 29/7—25/8/52.**H/I.**

BOILERS:
1687.
8214 *(new)* 19/1/29.
7893 *(ex4048)* 18/1/36.
8347 *(ex4059)* 1/7/39.
8750 *(ex8887)* 21/10/49.
8750 reno.21650 25/8/52.

SHED:
New England.

RENUMBERED:
4280 19/4/24.
8879 30/9/46.
68879 17/4/48.

CONDEMNED: 20/9/55.
Into Don. for cut up 20/9/55.

4281

Doncaster 1216.

To Traffic 12/1908.

REPAIRS:
Don. 28/2—24/6/22.**G.**
Don. 26/3—30/5/25.**G.**
Don. 10/1—16/3/28.**G.**
Don. 27/7—15/11/30.**G.**
Don. 27/8—29/10/32.**G.**
Don. 26/12/34—9/2/35.**G.**
Don. 18/3—2/4/38.**G.**
Don. 5/12/40—18/1/41.**G.**
Don. 31/1—19/2/44.**G.**
Don. 21/5—20/6/47.**G.**
Don. 18/4—18/5/50.**G.**
Don. 20/2—19/3/53.**G.**

BOILERS:
6935.
1645 *(ex1243)* 24/6/22.
8436 *(new)* 15/11/30.
8650 *(ex4248)* 2/4/38.
8477 *(ex8820)* 18/5/50.
21664 19/3/53.

SHEDS:
King's Cross.
New England 17/4/35.
Colwick 15/8/54.

RENUMBERED:
4281 30/5/25.
8880 1/12/46.
68880 18/5/50.

CONDEMNED: 17/8/56.
Into Don. for cut up 17/8/56.

4282

Doncaster 1217.

To Traffic 12/1908.

REPAIRS:
Don. 21/10—13/12/19.**G.**
Don. 28/2—2/8/24.**G.**
Don. 14/4—15/6/27.**G.**
Don. 28/2—25/5/29.**G.**
Don. 9/5—15/8/31.**G.**
Don. 8/12/33—10/2/34.**G.**
Don. 24/6—18/7/36.**G.**
Don. 5/9—25/11/39.**G.**
Don. 8/1—12/2/44.**G.**
Str. 26/4—29/6/47.**G.**
Str. 25/1—3/5/50.**G.**
Don. 9/5—5/6/53.**G.**

BOILERS:
6936.
8655 *(new)*10/2/34.
8262 *(ex8861)* 29/6/47.
8654 *(ex8776)* 3/5/50.
21672 5/6/53.

SHED:
King's Cross.

RENUMBERED:
4282 2/8/24.
8881 24/10/46.
68881 3/5/50.

CONDEMNED: 9/12/55.
Into Don. for cut up 9/12/55.

From July 1942 until January 1946, wartime conditions caused only NE to be put on. Engines repaired at Stratford had it applied in $7^{1}/_{2}$in. letters, as had been done for LNER.

Engines repaired at Doncaster had their NE increased to 12in. size, still in shaded transfers, except Departmental No.3980 which had $7^{1}/_{2}$in. for both letters and numbers.

In many instances, before LNER was restored, the 1946 renumbering took effect with J52 class being allocated 8757 to 8889. Much of this change was done at sheds by local painters, No.8857 being changed from 4258 on Sunday 28th April 1946 at Doncaster (Carr) engine shed.

When Stratford reverted to putting LNER on they dropped the size of the numbers to 7½in. because by August 1946 they only had limited stocks of 12in. numbers. No.4231 was ex works 17th August 1946 in this style, but on Friday 15th November 1946 was renumbered 8830 at King's Cross shed. Note the open Ramsbottom safety valves surviving to 3rd October 1948 on a boiler which started work in September 1908.

Some shed renumberings were not a good job even when shaded transfers were used. No.4284 had only NE from its 4th August 1945 repair at Stratford (*see* opposite, top) although obscured by dirt, when on Saturday 21st September 1946 Hornsey shed changed it to 8883 and to 7½in. figures. Neither spacing nor position showed good judgement, but it stayed that way until it went to Stratford 2nd December 1948.

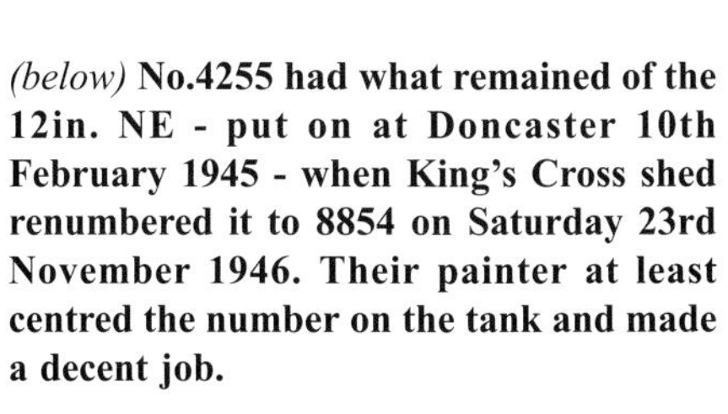
(below) **No.4255 had what remained of the 12in. NE - put on at Doncaster 10th February 1945 - when King's Cross shed renumbered it to 8854 on Saturday 23rd November 1946. Their painter at least centred the number on the tank and made a decent job.**

Ex Stratford 18th May 1946 from a General repair, No.8770 (ex3968) was accorded orthodox treatment of $7^1/_2$in. LNER and 12in. numbers.

No.8786, ex Doncaster works 13th May 1947, was in the new style painted and unshaded Gill sans but with modified figure 6, size and position were unchanged.

Out of Doncaster works on 28th January 1948, sizes, style and position were the same but with LNER replaced by BRITISH RAILWAYS and with Regional prefix E to the number 8788. During early 1948 seven more of the class got the prefix, four from Doncaster: E8819 (28th January), E8795 (26th February), E8823 (27th February), E8855 (8th March); and three from Stratford: E8829 (10th February), E8791 (12th March), E8764 (14th March).

4283

Doncaster 1218.

To Traffic 12/1908.

REPAIRS:
Don. 16/3—28/5/21.**G**.
Don. 16/2—2/5/25.**G**.
Don. 23/7—29/9/28.**G**.
Don. 14/3—30/5/31.**G**.
Don. 11/6—4/8/34.**G**.
Don. 19/12/36—9/1/37.**G**.
Don. 28/12/39—5/2/40.**G**.
Don. 11/6—12/7/42.**G**.
Don. 7/4—6/5/44.**G**.
Don. 9/10—2/11/46.**G**.
Don. 14/2—12/3/49.**G**.
Don. 13/2—6/3/52.**G**.
Don. 29/9—29/10/54.**G**.
Don. 10—29/8/56.**N/C**.
Don. 11/1/58. *Not Repaired.*

BOILERS:
6937.
1256 *(ex1256 & sp.)* 28/5/21.
8479 *(new)* 30/5/31.
8742 *(new)* 9/1/37.
7893 *(ex4280)* 5/2/40.
8743 *(ex3966)* 12/7/42.
8437 *(ex3980)* 6/5/44.
7892 *(ex4245)* 2/11/46.
21643 6/3/52.
21695 *(ex68871)* 29/10/54.

SHEDS:
Ardsley.
Colwick 22/6/26.
Woodford Halse 28/11/31.
Colwick 21/2/33.

RENUMBERED:
4283 2/5/25.
8882 15/9/46.
68882 12/3/49.

CONDEMNED: 27/1/58.
Cut up at Doncaster.

4284

Doncaster 1219.

To Traffic 12/1908.

REPAIRS:
Don. 7/3—7/5/21.**G**.
Don. 24/8—14/11/25.**G**.
Don. 2/3—29/6/29.**G**.
Don. 23/4—6/8/32.**G**.
Don. 2/5—13/6/36.**G**.
Don. 28/3—11/5/40.**G**.
Str. 15/6—4/8/45.**G**.
Str. 2—26/12/48.**G**.
Str. 9/6—29/7/50.**G**.

BOILERS:
6938.
6940 *(ex1286)* 7/5/21.
8262 *new)* 29/6/29.
8216 *(ex4240)* 13/6/36.
9495 *(new)* 4/8/45.
8655 *(ex8864)* 29/7/50.

SHEDS:
Ardsley.
Colwick 22/6/26.
Hornsey 1/11/33.
Annesley 19/10/52.
Hornsey 23/11/52.

RENUMBERED:
4284 14/11/25.
8883 21/9/46.
68883 25/12/48.

CONDEMNED: 26/9/55.
Into Don. for cut up 26/9/55.

4285

Doncaster 1220.

To Traffic 12/1908.

REPAIRS:
Don. 3/6—24/9/21.**G**.
Don. 13/8—20/12/24.**G**.
Don. 2/7—30/8/26.**G**.
Don. 16/3—10/11/28.**G**.
Don. 3/12/31—13/2/32.**G**.
Don. 5/7—3/8/35.**G**.
Don. 11/9—2/12/39.**G**.
Don. 15/5—10/6/44.**G**.
Str. 29/2—4/6/48.**G**.
Str. 17/5—30/6/50.**C/H**.
Str. 21/5—4/7/52.**G**.

BOILERS:
6939.
8201 *(new)* 10/11/28.
8749 *(ex8764)* 4/6/48.
21776 *(new)* 4/7/52.

SHEDS:
Hornsey.
King's Cross 16/10/46.
New England 6/9/53.

RENUMBERED:
4285 20/12/24.
8884 21/9/46.
68884 4/6/48.

CONDEMNED: 14/9/55.
Into Don. for cut up 14/9/55.

4286

Doncaster 1221.

To Traffic 1/1909.

REPAIRS:
Don. 12/1—27/3/20.**G**.
Don. 28/11/24—14/2/25.**G**.
Don. 8/3—3/8/28.**G**.
Don. 14/4—11/10/30.**G**.
Don. 26/10—9/12/33.**G**.
Don. 26/4—30/5/36.**G**.
Don. 17/10—5/11/38.**G**.
Don. 3—31/3/41.**G**.
Don. 9—26/2/44.**G**.
Don. 12/8—21/9/46.**G**.
Don. 15—23/6/47.**L**.
Don. 31/5—24/6/49.**G**.
Don. 10/7—7/8/53.**G**.

BOILERS:
6940.
1226 *(ex1233)* 27/3/20.
8434 *(new)* 11/10/30.
9502 *(new)* 21/9/46.
21625 *(ex68819)* 7/8/53.

SHEDS:
Doncaster.
Hatfield 9/12/51.
King's Cross 13/2/55.

RENUMBERED:
4286 14/2/25.
8885 19/7/46.
68885 24/6/49.

CONDEMNED: 18/9/56.
Into Don. for cut up 18/9/56.

4287

Doncaster 1222.

To Traffic 1/1909.

REPAIRS:
Don. 11/5—15/7/20.**G**.
Don. 15/12/24—7/3/25.**G**.
Don. 10/3—24/8/28.**G**.
Don. 8/10/30—6/1/31.**G**.
Don. 1/7—26/8/33.**G**.
Don. 30/7—7/9/35.**G**.
Don. 13/3—9/4/38.**G**.
Don. 2/9—5/10/40.**G**.
Don. 21/4—23/5/43.**G**.
Don. 31/12/45—16/2/46.**G**.
Don. 3/8—2/9/48.**G**.
Don. 26/8—27/9/51.**G**.
Don. 25/6—23/7/54.**H/I**.
Don. 13/11/57. *Not Repaired.*

BOILERS:
6941.
1262 *(ex1261 & sp.)* 15/7/20.
8472 *(new)* 6/1/31.
7888 *(ex4255)* 9/4/38.
8479 *(ex4203)* 23/5/43.
9810 *(new)* 2/9/48.
21631 27/9/51.

SHEDS:
Doncaster.
Retford 23/10/55.
Doncaster 27/11/55.

RENUMBERED:
4287 7/3/25.
8886 1/10/46.
68886 2/9/48.

CONDEMNED: 25/11/57.
Cut up at Doncaster.

4288

Doncaster 1223.

To Traffic 1/1909.

REPAIRS:
Don. 26/3—15/5/20.**G**.
Don. 29/9/23—9/2/24.**G**.
Don. 18/3—10/7/26.**G**.
Don. 6/12/28—11/5/29.**G**.
Don. 14/9—31/10/31.**G**.
Don. 12/5—21/7/34.**G**.
Don. 20/9—10/10/36.**G**.
Don. 13/7—16/9/39.**G**.
Don. 6/1—16/3/42.**G**.
Don. 29/1—19/2/44.**G**.
Don. 9/5—22/6/46.**G**.
Don. 16/8—17/9/48.**G**.
Don. 9—13/2/51.**N/C**.
Don. 13/8—5/9/51.**G**.
Don. 26/3—22/4/54.**G**.
Don. 23—27/4/54.**N/C**.
Don. 21/8/57. *Not Repaired.*

BOILERS:
6942.
1648 *(ex E1 864)* 9/2/24.
8256 *(new)* 11/5/29.
8475 *(ex3965)* 16/9/39.
8750 *(ex4206)* 19/2/44.
9814 *(new)* 17/9/48.
21699 *(new)* 5/9/51.
21680 22/4/54.

SHEDS:
Doncaster.
Colwick 27/5/37.

RENUMBERED:
4288 9/2/24.

From mid-March 1948 the prefix was superseded by the figure 6 in the modified style used by the LNER but the number remained on the tanks. No.68796 was out of Stratford works on 6th May 1948. Note the array of seven lamp brackets on the rear of the bunker.

No.68826 was an oddity, wearing only NE from a 25th August 1945 'General' at Doncaster, it went to Stratford works for a Light repair on 24th May 1948. This photograph was taken 30th June 1948 and why LNER was put on is a mystery, especially with BR renumbering. It was not released back into traffic until 31st July 1948 which is its official date for BR number.

On 19th January 1946 No.4216 was ex Stratford still with only 7$^{1}/_{2}$in. NE. It was changed to 8815 at Hornsey shed on Sunday 6th October 1946 and on 30th September 1948 it went into Stratford for a Light repair. This did not include painting but its BR number was put on in 12in. shaded transfers and this curiosity was ex works 2nd November 1948, remaining so until 9th November 1949.

When Doncaster changed to adding a 6 instead of E to make the BR number, it put the number on the bunker instead of on the tank. Ex works 19th March 1948, No.68767 was the first in this style. At Stratford, the number was still applied to the tanks at least to July, but No.68777 (*see* page 33, centre), ex works 7th August 1948, had it on the bunker.

(below) **Late in 1949 - No.68792 was ex works 2nd December 1949 - the BR emblem in 15$^{1}/_{2}$in. size began to be used by both Doncaster and Stratford works and this became the final livery for the class.**

The emblem was handed so that the lion faced to the front on both sides of the engine.

(below) **For exhibition in Noel Park goods yard, Wood Green on 12th to 14th September 1958, King's Cross shed cleaned and painted No.68846. Full lining was applied and BR crests were put on. It was the only one to get either crests or lining.**

When No.68846 was withdrawn on 8th May 1959 it was sold to W.G.Smith for private preservation, and in working condition. It was then restored, as near as practicable to original state and was painted in the fully lined green livery in which it began work in May 1899.

The last J52 to have a General repair was No.68824, ex works 4th May 1955 from Doncaster. The last two to survive were Nos.68869 and 68875 both withdrawn from Ardsley shed on 20th March 1961. Three of the class being cut up at Doncaster works in the company of an 0-6-0 tender engine.

4288 cont./
8887 22/9/46.
68887 17/9/48.

CONDEMNED: 26/8/57.
Cut up at Doncaster.

4289

Doncaster 1224.

To Traffic 2/1909.

REPAIRS:
Don. 12/6—14/8/20.**G**.
Don. 24/7—8/9/23.**G**.
Don. 9/7—4/9/26.**G**.
Don. 31/8—7/12/29.**G**.
Don. 16/12/32—11/2/33.**G**.
Don. 21/8—26/10/35.**G**.
Don. 2/3—11/4/38.**G**.
Don. 25/8—5/10/40.**G**.
Don. 13/2—11/3/44.**G**.
Str. 23/9—21/11/47.**G**.
Str. 4/6—5/8/50.**G**.
Don. 17/11—18/12/53.**G**.
Don. 17/10/57. *Not Repaired.*

BOILERS:
6943.
8345 *(new)* 7/12/29.
8435 *(ex4235)* 11/4/38.
8421 *(ex8780)* 21/11/47.
8744 *(ex8878)* 5/8/50.
21623 *(ex68786)* 18/12/53.

SHEDS:
New England.
King's Cross 17/5/33.

RENUMBERED:
1289N 8/9/23.
4289 4/9/26.
8888 21/9/46.
68888 5/8/50.

CONDEMNED: 21/10/57.
Cut up at Doncaster.

4290

Doncaster 1225.

To Traffic 2/1909.

REPAIRS:
Don. 29/8—3/12/21.**G**.
Don. 18/9—28/11/25.**G**.
Don. 31/12/28—8/6/29.**G**.
Don. 3/9—22/10/32.**G**.
Don. 13/6—4/7/36.**G**.
Don. 10/7—13/8/38.**G**.
Don. 14/2—6/4/41.**G**.
Don. 28/6—14/8/43.**G**.
Str. 12/4—31/5/45.**G**.
Str. 18/10—23/11/48.**G**.
Str. 4/9—6/10/51.**G**.
Don. 26/5/55. *Not Repaired.*

BOILERS:
6944.
8259 *(new)* 8/6/29.
8425 *(ex4225)* 4/7/36.
8348 *(ex4267)* 13/8/38.
9496 *(new)* 31/5/45.
9497 *(ex8873)* 23/11/48.
21772 *(new)* 6/10/51.

SHEDS:
New England.
Colwick 2/12/30.
King's Cross 1/11/33.
Spital Bridge 8/2/53.

RENUMBERED:
4290 28/11/25.
8889 11/10/46.
68889 23/11/48.

CONDEMNED: 30/5/55.
Cut up at Doncaster.

Doncaster built twenty more, Nos.961 to 980, to the same design between July 1893 and October 1895. By Grouping Nos.970 and 977 had been rebuilt with 4ft 5in. diameter boilers to become J52 class. Of the other eighteen, Nos.964, 971, 972, 974, 975, 976 and 979 had condensing apparatus.

Twenty similar engines were built by Neilson & Co., Glasgow, Nos.1046 to 1060 and 1211 to 1215, from July 1896 to June 1897. Of these, only No.1060 had been rebuilt with a 4ft 5in. boiler to J52 standard at Grouping. Ten of them had condensing apparatus, Nos.1046, 1047, 1048, 1050, 1051, 1054, 1056, 1057, 1058 and 1059 when they became LNER property. Note that No.1054 has destination board brackets.

CLASS J 52 & J 53

3921

Doncaster 591.

To traffic 12/1892.

REPAIRS:
Don. ?/?—?/8/02.**G.**
Don. 16/4—12/7/19.**G.**
Don. 6/2—4/8/23.**G.**
Rebuilt to J52.
Don. 29/11/26—12/2/27.**G.**
Don. 3—31/5/30.**G.**
Don. 23/6—14/7/34.**G.**
Don. 8/7/39. *Not Repaired.*

BOILERS:
921.
929 *(ex929)* ?/8/02.
1476 *(ex J4 1035)* 4/8/23.
8421 *(new)* 31/5/30.

SHED:
Hornsey.

RENUMBERED:
3921 12/2/27.

CONDEMNED: 13/7/39.
Cut up at Doncaster.

3922

Doncaster 597.

To traffic 12/1892.

REPAIRS:
Don. ?/?—?/5/07.**G.**
Don. 26/8—6/11/20.**G.**
Don. 21/9/23—12/1/24.**G.**
Rebuilt to J52.
Don. 7/3—21/5/27.**G.**
Don. 20/9—1/11/30.**G.**
Don. 1—15/6/35.**G.**
Don. 6/1—3/2/40.**G.**
Don. 29/7—19/8/44.**G.**
Str. 16/9—24/11/45.**L.**
Str. 7/8—2/11/47.**G.**
Str. 5—24/11/50.**C/L.**
Str. 17/7—6/9/52.**G.**
Don. 18/11/54. *Not Repaired.*

BOILERS:
922.
926 *(ex926)* ?/5/07.
1608 *(ex E1 753)* 12/1/24.
8438 *(new)* 1/11/30.
8438 reno.21722 24/11/50.
21753 6/9/52.

SHEDS:
Hornsey.
King's Cross 18/11/51.

RENUMBERED:
922N 12/1/24.
3922 23/3/25.
8757 21/7/46.
68757 24/11/50.

CONDEMNED: 29/11/54.
Cut up at Doncaster.

3923

Doncaster 599.

To traffic 2/1893.

REPAIRS:
Don. ?/?—?/2/10.**G.**
Don. ?/?—?/6/18.**G.**
Don. 30/3—2/7/21.**G.**
Don. 11/2—30/8/24.**G.**
Rebuilt to J52.
Don. 19/9—29/11/27.**G.**
Don. 14/11/31—13/2/32.**G.**
Don. 18/7—22/8/36.**G.**
Don. 1/12/40—3/1/41.**G.**
Don. 7/12/44—27/1/45.**G.**
Str. 25/7—11/9/48.**G.**
Str. 19/7—1/9/50.**C/L.**
Don. 11/12/52—8/1/53.**G.**

BOILERS:
923.
975 *(ex975)* ?/2/10.
924 *(ex925 & spare)* ?/6/18.
1315 *(exJ4 368)* 30/8/24.
7903 *(new)* 29/11/27.
8745 *(ex4223)* 27/1/45.
8206 *(ex8862)* 11/9/48.
21749 8/1/53.

SHEDS:
Hornsey.
Colwick 28/9/52.

RENUMBERED:
3923 30/8/24.
8758 21/7/46.
68758 11/9/48.

CONDEMNED: 25/11/55.
Into Don. for cut up 25/11/55.

3924

Doncaster 600.

To traffic 2/1893.

REPAIRS:
Don. ?/?—?/1/03.**G.**
Don. ?/?—?/12/10.**G.**
Don. ?/?—?/8/18.**G.**
Don. 9/12/20—16/4/21.**G.**
Don. 21/11/23—24/3/24.**G.**
Rebuilt to J52.
Don. 24/11/27—4/2/28.**G.**
Don. 7—28/6/30.**G.**
Don. 22/7—5/8/33.**G.**

BOILERS:
924.
1755 *(ex964)* ?/1/03.
963 *(ex963)* ?/12/10.
972 *(ex1058 & spare)* ?/8/18.
6878 *(exJ4 1086)* 24/3/24.
7986 *(new)* 4/2/28.

SHED:
Doncaster .

RENUMBERED:
3924 24/3/24.

WITHDRAWN: 9/3/36.
To Service Stock 13/6/36.
At Doncaster Works.
CONDEMNED: 14/9/36.
Cut up at Doncaster.

3925

Doncaster 603.

To traffic 3/1893.

REPAIRS:
Don. ?/?—?/5/04.**G.**
Don. ?/?—?/4/15.**G.**
Don. 16/4—5/6/20.**G.**
Don. 31/5—6/9/23.**G.**
Don. 20/12/26—10/3/27.**G.**
Don. 5/2—5/7/30.**G.**
Rebuilt to J52.
Don. 21/2—16/3/35.**G.**
Don. 25/2—6/4/40.**G.**
Don. 6/4—13/5/44.**G.**
Str. 26/11/46—11/1/47.**G.**
Str. 15—24/2/47.**N/C.**
Str. 25/9—12/11/49.**C/H.**
Str. 8/4—12/5/51.**G.**

BOILERS:
925.
924 *(ex924)* ?/5/04.
1636 *(new)* ?/4/15.
8426 *(new)* 5/7/30.
7902 *(ex4060)* 6/4/40.
8203 *(ex8794)* 11/1/47.
21732 12/5/51.

SHEDS:
Hornsey.
Doncaster 28/9/52.
New England 25/1/53.
Spital Bridge 8/2/53.
New England 2/1/55.
Colwick 11/10/55.

RENUMBERED:
925N 6/9/23.
3925 10/3/27.
8759 28/7/46.
68759 12/5/51.

CONDEMNED: 15/7/56.
Into Don. for cut up 19/7/56.

3926

Doncaster 605.

To traffic 3/1893.

REPAIRS:
Don. ?/?—?/6/06.**G.**
Don. 2/2—3/4/20.**G.**
Don. 3/8—15/12/23.**G.**
Rebuilt to J52.
Don. 28/3—8/6/27.**G.**
Don. 17/9—7/11/31.**G.**
Don. 20/9—19/10/35.**G.**
Don. 5/3—15/4/40.**G.**
Don. 29/8—23/9/44.**G.**
Str. 24/5—17/8/47.**G.**
Str. 28/8—6/9/47.**N/C.**
Str. 2/2—10/3/51.**G.**

BOILERS:
926.
925 *(ex925)* ?/6/06.
353 15/12/23.
8495 *(new)* 7/11/31.
9157 *(new)* 15/4/40.
8349 *(ex8772)* 17/8/47.
21727 10/3/51.

SHEDS:
Hornsey.
Ardsley 25/9/44.
Doncaster 22/10/44.
King's Cross 15/9/46.

3926 cont./
Hornsey 16/10/46.
New England 31/8/52.

RENUMBERED:
926N 15/12/23.
3926 4/3/25.
8760 7/7/46.
68760 10/3/51.

CONDEMNED: 9/11/54.
Into Don. for cut up 9/11/54.

3927

Doncaster 608.

To traffic 4/1893.

REPAIRS:
Don. 27/5—21/8/20.**G**.
Don. 1/3—31/7/23.**G**.
Don. 11/3—15/10/26.**G**.
Don. 17/8—29/11/29.**G**.
Rebuilt to J52.
Don. 16/2—5/5/34.**G**.
Don. 21/1—6/3/39.**G**.
Don. 12/2—25/3/44.**G**.
Str. 21/12/45—9/2/46.**H**.
Str. 28/8—15/10/49.**G**.
Str. 23/3—19/4/52.**C/L**.
Str. 12/8—27/9/52.**H/I**.
Don. 17/12/53—6/1/54.**C/L**.
Don. 21/5/57. *Not Repaired.*

BOILERS:
927.
7128 *(ex G2 3696; domed; 4' 2½")* 15/10/26.
8343 *(new)* 29/11/29.
9498 *(new)* 9/2/46.
21754 27/9/52.

SHEDS:
Hornsey.
Doncaster 19/10/52.

RENUMBERED:
3927 15/10/26.
8761 5/5/46.
68761 15/10/49.

CONDEMNED: 27/5/57.
Cut up at Doncaster.

3928

Doncaster 612.

To traffic 5/1893.

REPAIRS:
Don. ?/?—11/3/16.**G**.
Don. 14/3—28/5/21.**G**.
Don. 31/7—15/11/24.**G**.
Don. 25/6—8/9/28.**G**.
Don. 14/5—4/6/32.**G**.

BOILERS:
928.
979 *(ex966)* 11/3/16.
7131 *(ex3966; domed: 4' 2½")* 8/9/28.

SHED:
Ardsley.

RENUMBERED:
3928 15/11/24.

CONDEMNED: 30/11/35. *To service stock Doncaster Works.*
Cut up at Doncaster 6/36.

3929

Doncaster 613.

To traffic 6/1893.

REPAIRS:
Don. ?/?—?/4/02.**G**.
Don. 10/4—5/6/20.**G**.
Don. 22/8/23—18/1/24.**G**.
Rebuilt to J52.
Don. 2/8—15/10/27.**G**.
Don. 3/3—2/7/30.**G**.
Don. 10/7—30/9/33.**G**.
Don. 5/7—1/8/36.**G**.
Don. 20/3—13/5/39.**G**.
Don. 16—30/8/41.**G**.
Don. 21/11—21/12/43.**G**.
Don. 26/7—7/9/46.**G**.
Don. 30/11—29/12/48.**G**.
Don. 17/7/51. *Not Repaired.*

BOILERS:
929.
1711 *(ex966)* ?/4/02.
974 *(ex974 & spare)* 5/6/20.
1612 *(exE1 883)* 18/1/24.
8427 *(new)* 2/7/30.
8422 *(ex4207)* 30/8/41.
9499 *(new)* 7/9/46.

SHEDS:
Bradford.
Doncaster 2/9/26.
Colwick 23/6/37.

RENUMBERED:
929N 18/1/24.
3929 15/10/27.
8762 14/7/46.
68762 29/12/48.

CONDEMNED: 6/8/51.
Cut up at Doncaster.

3930

Doncaster 615.

To traffic 6/1893.

REPAIRS:
Don. ?/?—?/11/07.**G**.
Don. ?/?—?/10/14.**G**.
Don. 30/6—21/8/20.**G**.
Don. 21/12/23—2/9/24.**G**.
Rebuilt to J52.
Don. 1/11/28—2/2/29.**G**.
Don. 6/2—26/3/32.**G**.
Don. 25/8—19/9/36.**G**.
Don. 28/9—2/11/40.**G**.
Don. 27/2—10/4/43.**G**.
Don. 12/1—10/2/45.**G**.
Don. 24/2—3/3/45.**L**.
Don. 26/5—24/6/47.**G**.
Don. 21/9/50. *Not Repaired.*

BOILERS:
930.
970 *(ex970 & spare)* ?/11/07.
962 *(ex962)* ?/10/14.
1527 *(exC12 1520)* 2/9/24.
1228 *(ex4256)* 2/2/29.
8500 *(new)* 26/3/32.

SHEDS:
Bradford.
Doncaster 23/9/45.

RENUMBERED:
3930 2/9/24.
8763 26/5/46.

CONDEMNED: 2/10/50.
Cut up at Doncaster.

3961

Doncaster 618.

To traffic 7/1893.

REPAIRS:
Don. ?/?—?/10/16.**G**.
Don. 4/9—15/11/19.**G**.
Don. 1/3—29/6/23.**G**.
Don. 14/9—9/12/25.**G**.
Rebuilt to J52.
Don. 25/1—7/4/28.**G**.
Don. 25/10/30—31/1/31.**G**.
Don. 21/4—29/7/33.**G**.
Don. 2/2—7/3/36.**G**.
Don. 10/7—6/8/38.**G**.
Don. 31/3—3/5/41.**G**.
Don. 22/10—14/11/44.**G**.
Str. 12/1—14/3/48.**H**.
Str. 28/3—28/4/51.**G**.
Don. 14/10/54. *Not Repaired.*

BOILERS:
961.
970 *(ex930)* ?/10/16.
1657 *(exJ4 191)* 9/12/25.
1449 *(ex4060)* 7/4/28.
8474 *(new)* 31/1/31.
8749 *(ex4260)* 6/8/38.
8260 *(ex8795)* 14/3/48.
21731 28/4/51.

SHED:
King's Cross.

RENUMBERED:
3961 9/12/25.
8764 20/7/46.
E8764 14/3/48.
68764 28/4/51.

CONDEMNED: 1/11/54.
Cut up at Doncaster.

3962

Doncaster 619.

To traffic 8/1893.

REPAIRS:
Don. ?/?—?/11/13.**G**.
Don. 30/10/19—17/1/20.**G**.
Don. 21/12/23—6/9/24.**G**.
Rebuilt to J52.
Don. 14/2—4/5/27.**G**.
Don. 21/12/29—14/1/30.**G**.
Don. 9/2—10/7/33.**G**.
Don. 12—26/9/36.**G**.
Don. 10/11/39—13/1/40.**G**.
Don. 13/8—11/9/43.**G**.
Don. 12/3—20/4/47.**G**.
Don. 20/12/49—27/1/50.**G**.
Don. 17/11—11/12/52.**G**.

BOILERS:
962.
977 *(ex977 & spare)* ?/11/13.
963 *(ex924)* 17/1/20.
1441 *(ex J4 848)* 6/9/24.
8352 *(new)* 14/1/30.
7901 *(ex4060)* 26/9/36.
8433 *(ex4247)* 20/4/47.
8422 *(ex8792)* 27/1/50.
21656 11/12/52.

SHEDS:
Bradford.
Trafford Park 4/5/27.
New England 14/1/30.
Grantham 28/1/30.
New England 12/8/33.

3962 cont./
Colwick 16/1/55.

RENUMBERED:
3962 6/9/24.
8765 14/7/46.
68765 27/1/50.

CONDEMNED: 9/12/55.
Into Don. for cut up 9/12/55.

3963

Doncaster 623.

To traffic 8/1893.

REPAIRS:
Don. ?/?—?/9/09.**G**
Don. ?/?—?/7/13.**G**.
Don. 4/10/21—2/1/22.**G**.
Don. 24/8—21/11/25.**G**.
Don. 12/3—18/8/28.**G**.
Don. 16/5—13/9/32.**G**.
Rebuilt to J52.
Don. 28/6—18/7/36.**G**.
Don. 30/6—20/7/40.**G**.
Don. 28/7—19/8/44.**G**.
Don. 8/3—22/4/48.**G**.

BOILERS:
963.
930 *(ex930)* ?/9/09.
1498 *(new)* ?/7/13.
8521 *(new)* 13/9/32.

SHEDS:
Copley Hill.
Ardsley 9/1/28.
Copley Hill 5/12/28.
Ardsley 11/4/43.
Retford 7/12/48.
Doncaster 18/3/51.

RENUMBERED:
3963 21/11/25.
8766 7/7/46.
68766 22/4/48.

CONDEMNED: 23/1/52.
Into Don. for cut up 23/1/52.

3964

Doncaster 627.

To traffic 10/1893.

REPAIRS:
Don. ?/?—?/10/00.**G**.
Don. ?/?—?/5/09.**G**.
Don. 26/1—3/4/20.**G**.
Don. 26/7—8/11/23.**G**.
Don. 18/1—8/4/27.**G**.
Rebuilt to J52.
Don. 25/10/30—17/1/31.**G**.
Don. 17/11—15/12/34.**G**.
Don. 30/6/39. *Not Repaired.*

BOILERS:
1755.
964 *(new)* ?/10/00.
1056 *(ex1056)* ?/5/09.
961 *(ex961 & spare)* 3/4/20.
1203 *(ex4240)* 8/4/27.
8473 *(new)* 17/1/31.

SHEDS:
Hornsey *at* 6/5/24.
King's Cross *after* 2/5/25.
Hornsey *at* 1/1/35.
Doncaster 30/6/39.

RENUMBERED:
964N 8/11/23.
3964 ?/3/25.

CONDEMNED: 15/8/39.
Used temporarily as service stock at Doncaster works but cut up by July 1940.

3965

Doncaster 629.

To traffic 11/1893.

REPAIRS:
Don. ?/?—?/7/01.**G**.
Don. ?/?—?/8/14.**G**.
Don. 21/10/20—26/2/21.**G**.
Don. 27/5—15/11/24.**G**.
Don. 2/12/27—4/3/28.**G**.
Don. 18/11/30—6/2/31.**G**.
Rebuilt to J52.
Don. 27/1—31/3/34.**G**.
Don. 25/7—29/8/36.**G**.
Don. 16/1—25/2/39.**G**.
Don. 19/5—21/6/41.**G**.
Don. 10/7—7/8/43.**G**.
Don. 2/4—11/5/46.**G**.
Don. 16/2—19/3/48.**G**.
Don. 19/11/50. *Not Repaired.*

BOILERS:
1750.
965 *(new?)* ?/7/01.
1635 *(new)* ?/8/14.
8475 *(new)* 6/2/31.
8215 *(ex4213)* 25/2/39.
8751 *(ex4264)* 7/8/43.
9504 *(new)* 11/5/46.

SHED:
Colwick.

RENUMBERED:
3965 15/11/24.
8767 11/5/46.
68767 19/3/48.

CONDEMNED: 4/12/50.
Cut up at Doncaster.

3966

Doncaster 630.

To traffic 12/1893.

REPAIRS:
Don. ?/?—?/3/01.**G**.
Don. ?/?—?/3/10.**G**.
Don. ?/?—?/8/15.**G**.
Don. 5/7—15/10/21.**G**.
Don. 10/11/24—30/5/25.**G**.
Don. 25/11/27—21/1/28.**G**.
Rebuilt to J52.
Don. 11/10—13/12/30.**G**.
Don. 14/2—5/5/34.**G**.
Don. 14/10—7/11/36.**G**.
Don. 5/10—18/11/39.**G**.
Don. 13/5—6/6/42.**G**.
Don. 29/10—18/11/44.**G**.
Don. 2/1—22/2/47.**G**.
Don. 21/12/48—22/1/49.**G**.
Don. 4/9—4/10/51.**G**.
Don. 6/4—11/5/54.**G**.
Don. 12—14/5/54.**N/C**.
Don. 25/10/57. *Not Repaired.*

BOILERS:
1711.
966 *(new?)* ?/3/01.
979 *(ex979)* ?/3/10.
111 *(ex111)* ?/8/15.
7131 *(ex G1 940;domed; 4' 2½")* 30/5/25.
7983 *(new)* 21/1/28.
8742 *(new)* 5/5/34.
8212 *(ex4239)* 7/11/36.
8743 *(ex4208)* 18/11/39.
8657 *(ex3977)* 6/6/42.
8743 *(ex4283)* 18/11/44.
9503 *(ex8844)* 22/1/49.
21632 4/10/51.
21627 11/5/54.

SHED:
Colwick.

RENUMBERED:
3966 30/5/25.
8768 14/7/46.
68768 22/1/49.

CONDEMNED: 25/10/57.
Cut up at Doncaster.

3967

Doncaster 636.

To traffic 12/1893.

REPAIRS:
Don. ?/?—?/10/16.**G**.
Don. 16/4—21/6/19.**G**.
Don. 23/10/22—28/2/23.**G**.
Don. 6/4—3/7/26.**G**.
Don. 2/9/29—4/1/30.**G**.
Rebuilt to J52.
Don. 5/6—9/9/33.**G**.
Don. 29/7—14/8/37.**G**.
Don. 9/11—7/12/40.**G**.
Don. 2—18/9/43.**G**.
Don. 20/3—21/4/45.**G**.
Don. 22/3—10/5/48.**G**.
Don. 26/10—16/11/51.**G**.

BOILERS:
967.
964 *(ex969)* ?/10/16.
8349 *(new)* 4/1/30.
7982 *(ex4206)* 14/8/37.
21635 16/11/51.

SHEDS:
Bradford.
Doncaster 23/9/45.

RENUMBERED:
3967 3/7/26.
8769 7/7/46.
68769 8/5/48.

CONDEMNED: 23/9/55.
Into Don. for cut up 23/9/55.

3968

Doncaster 640.

To traffic 1/1894.

REPAIRS:
Don. ?/?—?/9/02.**G**.
Don. ?/?—?/11/13.**G**.
Don. 14/6—24/9/21.**G**.
Don. 7/11/23—1/3/24.**G**.
Rebuilt to J52.
Don. 7/6—26/8/26.**G**.
Don. 16/10—30/11/29.**G**.
Don. 23/1—24/6/32.**G**.
Don. 15/9—20/10/34.**G**.
Don. 12/2—27/3/37.**G**.
Don. 29/9—2/12/39.**G**.
Don. 25/8—2/10/43.**G**.
Str. 7/4—18/5/46.**G**.
Str. 5/12/49—28/1/50.**G**.
Don. 18/7/53. *Not Repaired.*

3968 cont./
BOILERS:
968.
1750 *(ex965)* ?/9/02.
976 *(ex976)* ?/11/13.
7092 *(exJ4 1036)* 1/3/24.
8522 *(new)* 24/6/32.
8346 *(ex4235)* 18/5/46.
7981 *(ex8774)* 28/1/50.

SHEDS:
Ardsley.
Gorton 18/2/27.
Wigan ?/?/?.
Gorton 2/7/28.
Trafford Park 27/8/28.
King's Cross 30/11/29.
Hornsey 25/11/51.
Sheffield 19/10/52.
Ardsley 25/1/53.

RENUMBERED:
3968 1/3/24.
8770 18/5/46.
68770 28/1/50.

CONDEMNED: 3/8/53.
Cut up at Doncaster.

3969

Doncaster 643.

To traffic 2/1894.

REPAIRS:
Don. ?/?—?/8/10.**G.**
Don. ?/?—?/1/16.**G.**
Don. 23/5—20/8/21.**G.**
Don. 26/9—20/12/24.**G.**
Don. 4/12/28—15/1/29.**G.**
Don. 7/5—17/9/32.**G.**
Rebuilt to J52.
Don. 6/4—18/5/35.**G.**
Don. 18/11—18/12/37.**G.**
Don. 11—28/7/40.**G.**
Don. 3/9—16/10/43.**G.**
Str. 22/2—26/3/46.**G.**
Str. 27/3—29/4/49.**G.**
Str. 29/4—7/6/52.**G.**

BOILERS:
969.
964 *(ex964)* ?/8/10.
1634 *(new)* ?/1/16.
8518 *(new)* 17/9/32.
8427 *(ex3972)* 26/3/46.
8493 *(ex8784)* 29/4/49.
21775 *(new)* 7/6/52.

SHEDS:
Hornsey.
King's Cross 15/4/32.
New England 6/9/53.

RENUMBERED:
3969 20/12/24.
8771 24/3/46.
68771 29/4/49.

CONDEMNED: 10/10/55.
Into Don. for cut up 10/10/55.

3970

Doncaster 647.

To traffic 3/1894.

REPAIRS:
Don. ?/?—?/2/03.**G.**
Don. 12/10—17/12/21.**G.**
Rebuilt to J52.
Don. 15/11/24—27/2/25.**G.**
Don. 11/2—27/7/29.**G.**
Don. 27/8—19/11/32.**G.**
Don. 15/6—27/7/35.**G.**
Don. 3—22/1/38.**G.**
Don. 17/10—23/11/40.**G.**
Don. 1/5—3/6/44.**G.**
Str. 19/4—14/6/47.**G.**
Str. 4/2—13/5/50.**G.**
Str. 27/10—29/11/52.**C/L.**
Don. 15/8/54. *Not Repaired.*

BOILERS:
970.
1054 *(ex1054)* ?/2/03.
1054 reno.67 ?/2/03.
6937 *(ex1283)* 17/12/21.
7084 *(ex3978)* 27/7/29.
8654 *(new)* 19/11/32.
8349 *(ex3967)* 22/1/38.
8652 *(ex8803)* 14/6/47.
8745 *(ex68830)* 13/5/50.
8745 reno.21755 29/11/52.

SHEDS:
Hornsey *at* 12/21 *&* 12/23.
King's Cross 8/2/32.

RENUMBERED:
3970 27/2/25.
8772 20/7/46.
68772 13/5/50.

CONDEMNED: 6/9/54.
Cut up at Doncaster.

3971

Doncaster 657.

To traffic 8/1894.

REPAIRS:
Don. ?/?—?/9/08.**G.**
Don. 8/4—16/7/21.**G.**
Don. 4/9—29/11/24.**G.**
Don. 16/3—16/11/28.**G.**
Rebuilt to J52.
Don. 14/3—2/7/32.**G.**
Don. 4—25/7/36.**G.**
Don. 16/10—16/11/40.**G.**
Don. 10—28/10/44.**G.**
Str. 12/8—5/10/46.**G.**
Str. 5/6—30/7/49.**G.**
Don. 30/3/53. *Not Repaired.*

BOILERS:
971.
1497 *(new)* ?/9/08.
8200 *(new)* 16/11/28.
7891 *(ex8794)* 30/7/49.

SHEDS:
Hornsey.
Colwick 28/9/52.

RENUMBERED:
3971 29/11/24.
8773 28/7/46.
68773 30/7/49.

CONDEMNED: 13/4/53.
Cut up at Doncaster.

3972

Doncaster 658.

To traffic 9/1894.

REPAIRS:
Don. ?/?—?/8/08.**G.**
Don. 4/6—24/9/21.**G.**
Don. 21/9—22/12/23.**G.**
Rebuilt to J52.
Don. 28/3—28/5/27.**G.**
Don. 25/1—20/4/29.**G.**
Don. 1/12/33—7/3/34.**G.**
Don. 8/8—17/9/38.**G.**
Don. 1—29/8/42.**G.**
Str. 24/1—9/3/46.**G.**
Str. 30/10—10/12/49.**G.**
Str. 26/1/50.**N/C.**
Don. 7/7/53. *Not Repaired.*

BOILERS:
972.
922 *(ex922)* ?/8/08.
6917 *(exE1 835)* 22/12/23.
8657 *(new)* 7/3/34.
8440 *(ex4237)* 17/9/38.
8427 *(ex3929)* 29/8/42.
7981 *(ex4274)* 9/3/46.
8522 *(ex8805)* 10/12/49.

SHEDS:
Hornsey.
Ardsley 19/10/52.
Doncaster 23/11/52.

RENUMBERED:
972N 22/12/23.
3972 28/5/27.
8774 28/7/46.
68774 10/12/49.

CONDEMNED: 20/7/53.
Cut up at Doncaster.

3973

Doncaster 659.

To traffic 10/1894.

REPAIRS:
Don. ?/?—?/12/10.**G.**
Don. 28/1—3/4/20.**G.**
Don. 18/4—28/7/23.**G.**
Don. 14/1—3/4/26.**G.**
Rebuilt to J52.
Don. 16/1—29/6/29.**G.**
Don. 23/12/31--5/3/32.**G.**
Don. 21/6—20/7/35.**G.**
Don. 15/2—2/5/36.**L.**
Don. 1—28/5/38.**G.**
Don. 15/12/40—11/1/41.**G.**
Don. 8—21/4/41.**L.**
Don. 18/11—11/12/43.**G.**
Don. 24/4—18/5/46.**G.**
Don. 15/1—4/2/49.**G.**

BOILERS:
973.
969 *(ex969)* ?/12/10.
1058 *(ex1056 & spare)* 3/4/20.
1105 *(exJ4 165)* 3/4/26.
8263 *(new)* 29/6/29.
8472 *(ex4287)* 28/5/38.
8426 *(ex4268)* 18/5/46.
8437 *(ex8846)* 4/2/49.

SHED:
Doncaster .

RENUMBERED:
3973 3/4/26.
8775 18/5/46.
68775 4/2/49.

CONDEMNED: 14/7/52.
Into Don. for cut up 14/7/52.

3974

Doncaster 660.

To traffic 11/1894.

REPAIRS:
Don. ?/?—?/8/15.**G.**
Don. 13/10—27/11/20.**G.**

The class was completed by Nos.111 and 155, built at Doncaster in August 1897. Ivatt introduced some detail differences from the previous fifty Stirling engines. They had steel instead of wooden sandwich front buffer beams. There were no lightening holes in the frames, and front sandboxes were now hopper shaped. No.155 had been 155A since 22nd November 1906.

Although remaining J53 class, from April 1925, five acquired domed boilers and Ivatt style Ramsbottom safety valves. These were 4ft $2^1/_2$in. boilers taken from 0-4-4 tank engines which had been withdrawn. Those so fitted were Nos.4046 (April 1925 to February 1931); 3966 (May 1925 to January 1928); 4211 (September 1925 to June 1932); 3927 (October 1926 to November 1929). All four then changed to a 4ft 5in. boiler and became J52 class. No.4046 was the first to have cab handrails of equal height, which then became the standard. It was the only J53 noted with a whistle mounted on the cab roof.

The 4ft $2^1/_2$in. boiler from No.3966 was put on No.3928, ex works 8th September 1928, and it was the only one not to be rebuilt to J52. It was also the only J53 to get plating behind the coal rails - on 4th June 1932. J53 class became extinct with its June 1936 scrapping but it was Service Stock from 30th November 1935.

3974 cont./
Don. 17/5—29/11/24.**G.**
Rebuilt to J52.
Don. 10/10—26/11/27.**G.**
Don. 8/6—5/9/31.**G.**
Don. 21/6—27/7/35.**G.**
Don. 19/9—25/11/39.**G.**
Don. 17/4—29/5/43.**G.**
Str. 7/3—27/4/46.**G.**
Str. 6/11—23/12/49.**G.**
Don. 14/10/53. *Not Repaired.*

BOILERS:
974.
1055 *(ex1055)* ?/8/15.
183 *(exJ4 1158)* 29/11/24.
7902 *(new)* 26/11/27.
6879 *(ex4246)* 27/7/35.
8654 *(ex4207)* 27/4/46.
9643 *(new)* 23/12/49.

SHEDS:
Hornsey.
Ardsley 19/10/52.
Doncaster 23/11/52.

RENUMBERED:
3974 29/11/24.
8776 27/4/46.
68776 23/12/49.

CONDEMNED: 26/10/53.
Cut up at Doncaster.

3975

Doncaster 661.

To traffic 12/1894.

REPAIRS:
Don. ?/?—?/2/09.**G.**
Don. ?/?—?/2/15.**G.**
Don. 13/10—27/11/20.**G.**
Don. 9/6—18/10/24.**G.**
Don. 31/12/27—15/3/28.**G.**
Don. 17/10—22/12/31.**G.**
Rebuilt to J52.
Don. 5/4—9/5/36.**G.**
Don. 10/8—14/9/40.**G.**
Don. 30/11/44—6/1/45.**G.**
Str. 7/6—7/8/48.**G.**
Str. 20/12/49—10/2/50.**C/L.**
Str. 10—17/3/51.**C/L.**
Str. 2/11/51—19/1/52.**H/I.**
Str. 6—24/5/52.**C/L.**
Don. 22/11/54. *Not Repaired.*

BOILERS:
975.
971 *(ex971)* ?/2/09.
1637 *(new)* ?/2/15.
8497 *(new)* 22/12/31.
8201 *(ex8884)* 7/8/48.
8201 reno 21729 17/3/51.

SHEDS:
Hornsey.
Colwick 19/10/52.

RENUMBERED:
3975 18/10/24.
8777 28/7/46.
68777 7/8/48.

CONDEMNED: 29/11/54.
Cut up at Doncaster.

3976

Doncaster 662.

To traffic 12/1894.

REPAIRS:
Don. ?/?—?/5/11.**G.**
Don. 27/5—24/7/20.**G.**
Don. 13/2—18/10/24.**G.**
Rebuilt to J52.
Don. 3/5—11/8/26.**L.**
Don. 21/12/27—10/3/28.**G.**
Don. 3/7—3/10/31.**G.**
Don. 10/6—4/7/36.**G.**
Don. 24/10—21/12/40.**G.**
Str. 23/4—9/6/45.**G.**
Str. 13/12/48—22/2/49.**G.**
Str. 12/2—11/3/50.**C/L.**
Str. 9/3—19/4/52.**G.**
Don. 9—15/12/56.**N/C.**
Don. 3/7/57. *Not Repaired.*

BOILERS:
976.
973 *(ex973)* ?/5/11.
975 *(ex923)* 24/7/20.
308 *(exG1 769)* 18/10/24.
1123 *(ex4206)* 10/3/28.
8493 *(new)* 3/10/31.
8348 *(ex4290)* 9/6/45.
9159 *(ex8825)* 22/2/49.
21773 *(new)* 19/4/52.

SHEDS:
Hornsey.
Doncaster 28/9/52.

RENUMBERED:
3976 18/10/24.
8778 28/7/46.
68778 22/2/49.

CONDEMNED: 3/7/57.
Cut up at Doncaster.

3977

Doncaster 681.

To traffic 5/1895.

REPAIRS:
Don. ?/?—?/11/10.**G.**
Don. 11/4—2/9/22.**G.**
Rebuilt to J52.
Don. 2/10—12/12/25.**G.**
Don. 11/1—15/6/29.**G.**
Don. 16/11/32—18/3/33.**G.**
Don. 24/5—20/6/36.**G.**
Don. 2/12/38—7/1/39.**G.**
Don. 9/12/40—11/1/41.**G.**
Don. 28/4—12/6/43.**G.**
Don. 12/6—21/7/45.**G.**
Don. 7—31/10/47.**G.**
Don. 24/4—26/5/50.**G.**
Don. 18/4/53. *Not Repaired.*

BOILERS:
977.
1046 *(ex1046)* ?/11/10.
1516 *(exC12 1516)* 2/9/22.
8260 *(new)* 15/6/29.
8657 *(ex3972)* 7/1/39.
8202 *(ex4225 & spare)* 11/1/41.
8473 *(ex4248)* 12/6/43.
8255 *(ex4259)* 21/7/45.
8650 *(ex8880)* 26/5/50.

SHEDS:
Ardsley.
Colwick 26/6/26.
Doncaster 21/10/33.
Colwick 28/10/36.

RENUMBERED:
3977 12/12/25.
8779 7/7/46.
68779 26/5/50.

CONDEMNED: 27/4/53.
Cut up at Doncaster.

3978

Doncaster 682.

To traffic 6/1895.

REPAIRS:
Don. 20/7—14/8/20.**G.**
Don. 29/1—20/6/23.**G.**
Rebuilt to J52.
Don. 18/10—31/12/26.**G.**
Don. 8/6—22/11/29.**G.**
Don. 21/11/31—19/3/32.**G.**
Don. 27/4—7/7/34.**G.**
Don. 31/12/36—30/1/37.**G.**
Don. 21/6—27/7/40.**G.**
Don. 24/5—17/6/44.**G.**
Str. 23/7—13/9/47.**G.**
Str. 20/6—19/8/50.**G.**
Don. 11/1/54. *Not Repaired.*

BOILERS:
978.
7084 20/6/23.
8340 *(new)* 22/11/29.
8210 *(ex4202)* 30/1/37.
8421 *(ex3921)* 27/7/40.
9157 *(ex8760)* 13/9/47.
8436 *(ex8822)* 19/8/50.

SHEDS:
Ardsley.
King's Cross 6/7/26.
Grantham 22/7/51.

RENUMBERED:
3978 31/12/26.
8780 6/12/46.
68780 19/8/50.

CONDEMNED: 25/1/54.
Cut up at Doncaster.

3979

Doncaster 683.

To traffic 8/1895.

REPAIRS:
Don. ?/?—?/11/00.**G.**
Don. ?/?—?/7/09.**G.**
Don. 27/10/21—4/3/22.**G.**
Don. 19/11/24—13/2/25.**G.**
Don. 9/7—26/10/28.**G.**
Don. 25/5—2/11/32.**G.**
Rebuilt to J52.
Don. 30/12/36—23/1/37.**G.**
Don. 25/2—24/3/41.**G.**
Str. 4/4—18/5/45.**G.**
Str. 14/9—27/10/48.**G.**
Str. 5/12/50—20/1/51.**G.**
Don. 9/12/54. *Not Repaired.*

BOILERS:
979.
979 *(new)* ?/11/00.
1633 *(new)* ?/7/09.
8651 *(new)* 2/11/32.
8496 *(ex8809)* 27/10/48.
21724 20/1/51.

SHEDS:
Hornsey.
King's Cross 18/4/32.
Hornsey 19/11/32.
Colwick 28/9/52.

RENUMBERED:
3979 13/2/25.
8781 24/11/46.

3979 cont./
68781 27/10/48.

CONDEMNED: 13/12/54.
Cut up at Doncaster.

3980

Doncaster 684.

To traffic 10/1895.

REPAIRS:
Don. 11/1—24/5/19.**G**.
Don. 5/2—12/6/23.**G**.
Rebuilt to J52.
Don. 17/6—3/9/26.**G**.
Don. 20/9—18/10/30.**G**.
Don. 26/8—23/9/33.**G**.
Don. 23/9/36. *Not Repaired. Withdrawn & sent to Service Stock 9/11/36, at Doncaster works.*
Don. 7/10—2/12/39.**G**.
Don. 6—11/10/41.**L**.
Don. 5—12/9/42.**L**.
Don. 31/7—14/8/43.**G**.
Don. 27/1—3/2/45.**L**.
Don. 22—29/9/45.**L**.
Don. 20/9—5/10/46.**L**.
Don. 30/6—3/7/48.**G**.
Don. 27/6—1/7/49.**C/L**.
Don. 5—9/9/49.**C/L**.

BOILERS:
980.
1169 12/6/23.
8437 *(new)* 18/10/30.
8197 *(ex4226 & spare)* 14/8/43.

SHEDS:
Bradford.
Boston ?/?/?.
New England 3/1/30.
Doncaster works 9/11/36.

RENUMBERED:
3980 3/9/26.
8782 14/11/46.
68782 3/7/48.

WITHDRAWN: 9/11/36.

CONDEMNED: 23/6/50.
Cut up Doncaster 15/7/50.

4046

Neilson 5017.

To traffic 7/1896.

REPAIRS:
Don. ?/?—?/4/08.**G**.
Don. ?/?—?/12/18.**G**.
Don. 9/11/21—28/2/22.**G**.
Don. 8/12/24—4/4/25.**G**.
Don. 9/5—10/8/27.**G**.
Don. 30/9/30—11/2/31.**G**.
Rebuilt to J52.
Don. 26/7—7/9/35.**G**.
Don. 30/5—24/6/40.**G**.
Don. 18/1—24/3/45.**G**.
Don. 31/3—15/6/48.**G**.
Str. 6/1—21/2/52.**G**.

BOILERS:
1046.
1047 *(ex1047)* ?/4/08.
1057 *(ex1054)* ?/12/18.
6908 *(exG2 682;domed; 4' 2½")* 4/4/25.
8476 *(new)* 11/2/31.
8495 *(ex3926)* 24/6/40.
9637 *(new)* 15/6/48.
21725 *(ex68809)* 21/2/52.

SHEDS:
Hornsey.
Sheffield 19/10/52.
New England 25/1/53.
Spital Bridge 8/2/53.
New England 2/1/55.

RENUMBERED:
4046 4/4/25.
8783 7/12/46.
68783 15/6/48.

CONDEMNED: 3/10/55.
Into Don. for cut up 3/10/55.

4047

Neilson 5018.

To traffic 7/1896.

REPAIRS:
Don. ?/?—?/5/07.**G**.
Don. 24/6—4/9/20.**G**.
Don. 16/11/23—17/5/24.**G**.
Rebuilt to J52.
Don. 18/10/26—1/3/27.**G**.
Don. 15/8—12/10/29.**G**.
Don. 10/11/33—20/1/34.**G**.
Don. 4—26/3/38.**G**.
Don. 2/4—29/5/43.**G**.
Str. 3/5—9/6/45.**G**.
Str. 8—29/12/47.**L**.
Str. 23/2—6/3/49.**G**.
Str. 13/8—8/9/51.**C/L**.
Don. 5—29/1/53.**G**.
Don. 20/11/57. *Not Repaired.*

BOILERS:
1047.
1048 *(ex1048)* ?/5/07.
6955 *(exJ7 1030)* 17/5/24.
7887 *(new)* 1/3/27.
8342 *(ex4057)* 26/3/38.
8493 *(ex3976)* 9/6/45.
8348 *(ex8778)* 6/3/49.
8348 reno.21737 8/9/51.
21658 29/1/53.

SHEDS:
Hornsey.
Doncaster 28/9/52.

RENUMBERED:
4047 17/5/24.
8784 7/12/46.
68784 5/3/49.

CONDEMNED: 25/11/57.
Cut up at Doncaster.

4048

Neilson 5019.

To traffic 7/1896.

REPAIRS:
Don. ?/?—?/12/05.**G**.
Don. 1/7—18/9/20.**G**.
Don. 11/12/23—28/6/24.**G**.
Rebuilt to J52.
Don. 6/5—3/8/27.**G**.
Don. 19/10—21/11/31.**G**.
Don. 25/10—23/11/45.**G**.
Don. 31/12/39—20/2/40.**G**.
Don. 16/7—19/8/44.**G**.
Str. 27/3—17/5/46.**G**.
Str. 17/6—30/7/49.**G**.
Str. 29/8—1/10/49.**C/L**.
Str. 23/6—16/8/52.**C/L**.
Str. 12—29/10/52.**C/L**.
Don. 18/1—26/2/54.**G**.
Don. 22/12/57. *Not Repaired.*

BOILERS:
1048.
1050 *(ex1050)* ?/12/05.
971 *(ex975 & spare)* 18/9/20.
1423 *(exJ4 1125)* 28/6/24.
7893 *(new)* 3/8/27.
7898 *(ex4238)* 23/11/35.
8659 *(ex4055)* 20/2/40.
8427 *(ex8771)* 30/7/49.
8427 reno.21751 16/8/52.

SHEDS:
Hornsey.
Doncaster 28/9/52.
Colwick 30/10/55.

RENUMBERED:
4048 28/6/24.
8785 7/12/46.
68785 30/7/49.

CONDEMNED: 6/1/58.
Cut up at Doncaster.

4049

Neilson 5020.

To traffic 7/1896.

REPAIRS:
Don. ?/?—?/3/05.**G**.
Don. ?/?—?/4/16.**G**.
Don. 15/2—7/5/21.**G**.
Don. 14/8—2/11/23.**G**.
Rebuilt to J52.
Don. 10/12/25—27/2/26.**G**.
Don. 27/8—14/12/29.**G**.
Don. 11/11/33—3/2/34.**G**.
Don. 31/1—20/2/37.**G**.
Don. 16/10—16/11/40.**G**.
Don. 8—31/3/44.**G**.
Don. 10/4—5/5/45.**L**.
Don. 6/4—13/5/47.**G**.
Don. 15/9—13/10/50.**G**.

BOILERS:
1049.
968 *(ex968)* ?/3/05.
1214 *(ex1214 & spare)* ?/4/16.
6879 2/11/23.
8346 *(new)* 14/12/29.
8340 *(ex3978)* 20/2/37.
8256 *(ex4288)* 16/11/40.
8434 *(ex8885)* 13/5/47.
21623 13/10/50.

SHEDS:
Doncaster .
New England 14/1/51.

RENUMBERED:
1049N 2/11/23.
4049 27/2/26.
8786 16/12/46.
68786 13/10/50.

CONDEMNED: 23/11/53.
Into Don. for cut up 23/11/53.

4050

Neilson 5021.

To traffic 7/1896.

REPAIRS:
Don. ?/?—?/4/03.**G**.
Don. 23/9—20/11/20.**G**.

4050 cont./
Don. 13/2—8/9/23.**G**.
Rebuilt to J52.
Don. 15/1—1/4/27.**G**.
Don. 6/3—18/7/30.**G**.
Don. 10/8—22/9/34.**G**.
Don. 16/6—5/8/39.**G**.
Don. 14/2—18/3/44.**G**.
Str. 27/10—8/12/47.**G**.
Str. 8/6—26/8/50.**C/L**.
Str. 16/12/51—2/2/52.**G**.

BOILERS:
1050.
921 *(ex921)* ?/4/03.
1289 8/9/23.
8428 *(new)* 18/7/30.
8435 *(ex8888)* 8/12/47.
21744 2/2/52.

SHEDS:
Hornsey.
Colwick 28/9/52.

RENUMBERED:
1050N 8/9/23.
4050 23/3/25.
8787 8/12/46.
68787 26/8/50.

CONDEMNED: 19/10/55.
Into Don. for cut up 19/10/55.

4051

Neilson 5022.

To traffic 7/1896.

REPAIRS:
Don. ?/?—?/8/06.**G**.
Don. 11/11/19—28/2/20.**G**.
Don. 30/5—8/9/23.**G**.
Rebuilt to J52.
Don. 12/7/26—19/1/27.**G**.
Don. 20/5—7/8/30.**G**.
Don. 25/5—21/7/34.**G**.
Don. 21/3—13/5/39.**G**.
Don. 22/3—15/4/44.**G**.
Don. 1/12/47—28/1/48.**G**.
Str. 23/3—3/5/52.**G**.
Don. 24/12/54. *Not Repaired.*

BOILERS:
1051.
1049 *(ex1049)* ?/8/06.
363 *(exJ4 352)* 8/9/23.
6955 *(ex4047)* 19/1/27.
8430 *(new)* 7/8/30.
8429 *(ex4054)* 13/5/39.
8471 *(ex8793)* 28/1/48.
21774 *(new)* 3/5/52.

SHEDS:
Hornsey.
Colwick 28/9/52.

RENUMBERED:
1051N 8/9/23.
4051 19/1/27.
8788 14/12/46.
E8788 28/1/48.
68788 3/5/52.

CONDEMNED: 27/12/54.
Cut up at Doncaster.

4052

Neilson 5023.

To traffic 7/1896.

REPAIRS:
Don. ?/?—?/1/19.**G**.
Don. 14/5—2/7/20.**G**.
Don. 23/10/23—15/3/24.**G**.
Rebuilt to J52.
Don. 15/3—24/5/27.**G**.
Don. 6/7—4/10/30.**G**.
Don. 19/12/33—10/3/34.**G**.
Don. 25/2—10/4/37.**G**.
Don. 14/5—8/6/40.**G**.
Don. 1—22/2/41.**L**.
After collision.
Don. 14/7—15/8/43.**G**.
Don. 17/11/46—2/1/47.**G**.
Don. 13/6—15/7/49.**G**.

BOILERS:
1052.
968 *(ex1049 & spare)* ?/1/19.
6942 *(ex1288)* 15/3/24.
8656 *(new)* 10/3/34.

SHEDS:
Ardsley.
New England 18/6/26.

RENUMBERED:
4052 15/3/24.
8789 16/12/46.
68789 15/7/49.

CONDEMNED: 29/4/52.
Into Don. for cut up 29/4/52.

4053

Neilson 5024.

To traffic 7/1896.

REPAIRS:
Don. 22/7—29/10/21.**G**.
Don. 29/7—6/12/24.**G**.
Rebuilt to J52.
Don. 30/12/27—10/3/28.**G**.
Don. 17/3—26/9/30.**G**.
Don. 15/7—3/8/35.**G**.
Don. 2—28/1/39.**G**.
Don. 7/2—22/3/42.**L**.
Don. 11/10—9/11/42.**G**.
Don. 12/8—8/9/45.**G**.
Don. 21/3—21/4/49.**G**.
Don. 10/7—1/8/51.**C/L**.
Don. 12/9—10/10/52.**G**.

BOILERS:
1053.
1136 *(ex G1 939)* 6/12/24.
8432 *(new)* 26/9/30.
8430 *(ex4055)* 8/9/45.
21653 10/10/52.

SHEDS:
Bradford.
Ardsley 12/4/40.
Bradford 13/6/40.
Ardsley 15/12/40.
Bradford 21/1/45.
Ardsley 12/3/45.
Bradford 21/3/45.
Ardsley 1/5/45.

RENUMBERED:
4053 6/12/24.
8790 10/11/46.
68790 21/4/49.

CONDEMNED: 11/7/55.
Into Don. for cut up 11/7/55.

4054

Neilson 5025.

To traffic 7/1896.

REPAIRS:
Don. ?/?—?/11/12.**G**.
Don. ?/?—?/5/18.**G**.
Don. 18/12/20—9/4/21.**G**.
Don. 13/2—1/4/22.**L**.
Don. 21/3—18/10/24.**G**.
Rebuilt to J52.
Don. 5/2—22/4/27.**G**.
Don. 13/3—23/7/30.**G**.
Don. 13/4—16/6/34.**G**.
Don. 6—29/10/38.**G**.
Don. 10/8—25/9/43.**G**.
Str. 18/7—12/9/45.**G**.
Str. 15/1—12/3/48.**L**.
Str. 21/12/48—4/2/49.**G**.
Str. 30/4—8/5/52.**N/C**.
Str. 7/9—11/10/52.**G**.

BOILERS:
1054. *Boiler renewed 2/03 with same number.Old boiler reno.67 and put on engine No.970.*
1057 *(ex1057& spare)* ?/11/12.
1059 *(ex1057)* ?/5/18.
6918 *(exG1 830)* 18/10/24.
8429 *(new)* 23/7/30.
8214 *(ex4250)* 29/10/38.
8344 *(ex4271)* 25/9/43.
8216 *(ex4284)* 12/9/45.
9156 *(ex8853)* 4/2/49.
21777 *(new)* 11/10/52.

SHEDS:
Hornsey.
Colwick 19/10/52.

RENUMBERED:
4054 18/10/24.
8791 15/12/46.
E8791 12/3/48.
68791 4/2/49.

CONDEMNED: 8/11/54.
Into Don. for cut up 8/11/54.

4055

Neilson 5026.

To traffic 7/1896.

REPAIRS:
Don. ?/?—?/6/14.**G**.
Don. 3/8—2/10/20.**G**.
Don. 8/12/24—28/2/25.**G**.
Don. 13/10—23/12/27.**G**.
Rebuilt to J52.
Don. 29/10—23/12/30.**G**.
Don. 20/1—7/4/34.**G**.
Don. 19/8—19/9/36.**G**.
Don. 21/6—26/8/39.**G**.
Don. 4/3—4/4/42.**G**.
Don. 14/7—5/8/44.**G**.
Don. 13/3—3/4/47.**G**.
Don. 31/10—2/12/49.**G**.
Don. 3/6/52. *Not Repaired.*

WORKS CODES:- Cow - Cowlairs. Dar - Darlington. Don - Doncaster. Ghd - Gateshead. Gor - Gorton. Inv - Inverurie. Kit - Kittybrewster. RSH - Robert, Stephenson & Hawthorn. Str - Stratford. Yk - York.
REPAIR CODES:- **C/H** - Casual Heavy. **C/L** - Casual Light. **G** - General. **H**- Heavy. **H/I** - Heavy Intermediate. **L** - Light. **L/I** - Light Intermediate. **N/C** - Non-Classified.

4055 cont./
BOILERS:
1055.
1060 *(ex1060 & spare)* ?/6/14.
1496 *(ex155A & sp.)* 2/10/20.
7989 *(new)* 23/12/27.
8659 *(new)* 7/4/34.
8430 *(ex4051)* 26/8/39.
8214 *(ex4054)* 5/8/44.
8422 *(ex8762)* 3/4/47.
10515 *(new)* 2/12/49.

SHED:
Colwick.

RENUMBERED:
4055 28/2/25.
8792 10/11/46.
68792 2/12/49.

CONDEMNED: 9/6/52.
Cut up at Doncaster.

4056

Neilson 5027.

To traffic 7/1896.

REPAIRS:
Don. ?/?—?/1/08.**G**.
Don. ?/?—?/6/14.**G**.
Don. 29/1—24/4/20.**G**.
Don. 4/8—17/11/23.**G**.
Rebuilt to J52.
Don. 23/5—2/8/27.**G**.
Don. 11/10/30—10/1/31.**G**.
Don. 21/6—27/7/35.**G**.
Don. 6/1—11/2/39.**G**.
Don. 28/12/43—11/2/44.**G**.
Str. 24/7—5/10/47.**G**.
Str. 14/10—17/11/51.**G**.
Don. 17/5/56. *Not Repaired.*

BOILERS:
1056.
1058 *(ex1058)* ?/1/08.
930 *(ex963)* ?/6/14.
1255 *(ex1254)* 17/11/23.
8471 *(new)* 10/1/31.
7984 *(ex8864)* 5/10/47.
21738 17/11/51.

SHEDS:
Hornsey.
Frodingham 19/10/52.
Doncaster 21/6/53.
Ardsley 16/8/53.
New England 23/8/53.

RENUMBERED:
1056N 17/11/23.
4056 2/8/27.
8793 15/12/46.
68793 17/11/51.

CONDEMNED: 21/5/56.
Cut up at Doncaster.

4057

Neilson 5028.

To traffic 7/1896.

REPAIRS:
Don. ?/?—?/7/09.**G**.
Don. ?/?—?/5/17.**G**.
Don. 9/11/22—24/2/23.**G**.
Don. 8/2—29/5/26.**G**.
Rebuilt to J52.
Don. 9/7—30/11/29.**G**.
Don. 11/8—4/11/33.**G**.
Don. 5—29/1/38.**G**.
Don. 11/12/42—9/1/43.**G**.
Don. 11—31/1/43.**N/C**.
Str. 20/9—26/10/46.**G**.
Str. 30/11—29/12/47.**G**.
Str. 25/1—16/2/49.**C/H**.
Str. 18/3—27/4/51.**G**.
Don. 2/12/53. *Not Repaired.*

BOILERS:
1057.
1059 *(ex1059)* ?/7/09.
967 *(ex967)* ?/5/17.
1611 *(exJ55 620)* 29/5/26.
8342 *(new)* 30/11/29.
8203 *(ex4278)* 29/1/38.
7891 *(ex4231)* 26/10/46.
8494 *(ex8833)* 16/2/49.
21730 27/4/51.

SHEDS:
Hornsey.
Doncaster 28/9/52.

RENUMBERED:
4057 29/5/26.
8794 22/12/46.
68794 12/2/49.

CONDEMNED: 14/12/53.
Cut up at Doncaster.

4058

Neilson 5029.

To traffic 7/1896.

REPAIRS:
Don. ?/?—?/1/09.**G**.
Don. ?/?—?/3/14.**G**.
Don. 13/1—27/3/20.**G**.
Don. 26/1—28/4/23.**G**.
Don. 14/4—24/7/26.**G**.
Don. 5/10/29—22/1/30.**G**.
Rebuilt to J52.
Don. 13/7—25/8/34.**G**.
Don. 1/5—17/6/39.**G**.
Don. 1/5—3/6/44.**G**.
Don. 3/1—26/2/48.**G**.
Str. 13/3—4/5/50.**C/L**.
Str. 31/12/51—9/2/52.**G**.
Don. 23/11/55. *Not Repaired.*

BOILERS:
1058.
972 *(ex972)* ?/1/09.
1054 *(ex1054)* ?/3/14.
8350 *(new)* 22/1/30.
8260 *(ex3977)* 17/6/39.
8429 *(ex8788)* 26/2/48.
21746 9/2/52.

SHEDS:
Hornsey.
Doncaster 19/10/52.

RENUMBERED:
4058 *at shed* 13/2/25.
8795 22/12/46.
E8795 26/2/48.
68795 9/2/52.

CONDEMNED: 23/11/55.
Cut up at Doncaster.

4059

Neilson 5030.

To traffic 7/1896.

REPAIRS:
Don. ?/?—?/12/08.**G**.
Don. 4/9—23/12/22.**G**.
Don. 2/2—1/5/26.**G**.
Rebuilt to J52.
Don. 30/8—16/12/29.**G**.
Don. 15/6—4/8/34.**G**.
Don. 31/3—27/5/39.**G**.
Don. 9/1—12/2/44.**G**.
Str. 20/5—29/6/45.**L**.
Str. 17/1—6/5/48.**G**.
Str. 13/8—22/9/51.**G**.
Str. 17—19/12/51.**N/C**.

BOILERS:
1059.
1051 *(ex1051)* ?/12/08.
1168 *(exJ4 3734)* 1/5/26.
8347 *(new)* 16/12/29.
8478 *(ex4259)* 27/5/39.
9635 *(new)* 6/5/48.
21770 *(new)* 22/9/51.

SHEDS:
Hornsey.
Doncaster 19/10/52.

RENUMBERED:
4059 1/5/26.
8796 22/12/46.
68796 6/5/48.

CONDEMNED: 3/11/55.
Into Don. for cut up 3/11/55.

4060

Neilson 5031.

To traffic 7/1896.

REPAIRS:
Don. ?/?—?/11/10.**G**.
Don. 31/5—2/9/22.**G**.
Rebuilt to J52.
Don. 29/6—29/8/25.**G**.
Don. 19/7—8/10/27.**G**.
Don. 15/11/30—7/2/31.**G**.
Don. 28/7—21/10/33.**G**.
Don. 29/7—19/9/36.**G**.
Don. 1/5—17/6/39.**G**.
Don. 28/1—22/3/42.**G**.
Str. 26/4—16/6/45.**G**.
Str. 26/5—24/7/48.**G**.
Str. 12/12/51—25/1/52.**G**.

BOILERS:
1060.
923 *(ex923)* ?/11/10.
1449 2/9/22.
7901 *(new)* 8/10/27.
7902 *(ex3974)* 19/9/36.
7895 *(ex4217)* 17/6/39.
8495 *(ex8783)* 24/7/48.
21743 25/1/52.

SHEDS:
Hornsey.
King's Cross 11/3/30.
Spital Bridge 8/2/53.

RENUMBERED:
4060 29/8/25.
8797 23/12/46.
68797 24/7/48.

CONDEMNED: 3/11/55.
Into Don. for cut up 3/11/55.

4211

Neilson 5095.

To traffic 6/1897.

REPAIRS:
Don. ?/?—?/6/14.**G**.
Don. 19/5—2/9/22.**G**.
Don. 12/5—5/9/25.**G**.
Don. 1/3—12/12/28.**G**.

Apart from Nos.111 and 155A, all the others had sandboxes of rectangular shape at the front end. Until after Grouping the sand was delivered some distance ahead of where it could be most effective.

(above) **Starting in 1925, the front sandpipes were lengthened and curved round the brake hanger to put the sand just in front of the wheel.**

On all except Nos.3111 and 3155A, the brake pull rods were arranged outside the wheels. Vacuum brake was standard.

4211 cont./
Don. 9/4—4/6/32.**G**.
Rebuilt to J52.
Don. 9/3—6/4/35.**G**.
Don. 21/10—19/11/38.**G**.
Don. 28/7—24/8/41.**G**.
Don. 21/8—9/9/44.**G**.
Don. 9/10—7/11/47.**G**.
Don. 18/10—16/11/50.**G**.
Don. 25/10/54. *Not Repaired.*

BOILERS:
1211.
1213 *(ex1213)* ?/6/14.
1535 *(ex G2 765;domed; 4' 2½")* 5/9/25.
8520 *(new)* 4/6/32.
21624 16/11/50.

SHEDS:
New England.
Grantham 3/12/50.
Frodingham 7/12/52.
Colwick 17/5/53.

RENUMBERED:
4211 5/9/25.
8798 30/9/46.
68798 16/11/50.

CONDEMNED: 8/11/54.
Cut up at Doncaster.

4212

Neilson 5096.

To traffic 6/1897.

REPAIRS:
Don. ?/?—?/6/09.**G**.
Don. ?/?—?/5/18.**G**.
Don. 15/6—3/9/21.**G**.
Don. 14/7—31/10/25.**G**.
Rebuilt to J52.
Don. 22/9—1/12/28.**G**.
Don. 28/6—30/8/30.**G**.
Don. 17/9—26/11/32.**G**.
Don. 5/4—4/5/35.**G**.
Don. 28/10—20/11/37.**G**.
Don. 17/8—21/9/40.**G**.
Don. 1/4—6/5/44.**G**.
Str. 22/2—29/5/48.**G**.
Str. 27/2—31/3/51.**H/I**.
Don. 12/9/54. *Not Repaired.*

BOILERS:
1212.
1215 *(ex1215)* ?/6/09.
1212 *(ex1214)* ?/5/18.
303 *(exJ4 750)* 31/10/25.
8204 *(new)* 1/12/28.
8658 *(ex4216)* 20/11/37.
9636 *(new)* 29/5/48.
9636 reno.21728 31/3/51.

SHED:
King's Cross.

RENUMBERED:
4212 31/10/25.
8799 17/11/46.
68799 29/5/48.

CONDEMNED: 4/10/54. .
Cut up at Doncaster.

4213

Neilson 5097.

To traffic 6/1897.

REPAIRS:
Don. ?/?—?/8/13.**G**
Don. 9/3—16/6/21.**G**.
Don. 18/5—8/8/25.**G**.
Don. 15/10—21/12/27.**G**.
Don. 23/8—20/9/30.**G**.
Rebuilt to J52.
Don. 21/1—29/4/33.**G**.
Don. 19/1—1/2/36.**G**.
Don. 10/8—2/9/38.**G**.
Don. 18/4—31/5/41.**G**.
Don. 4—25/11/44.**G**.
Don. 23/9—6/10/45.**L**.
Don. 21/3—1/5/47.**G**.
Don. 22/8—22/9/50.**G**.
Don. 13/5—21/6/54.**G**.
Don. 10/7/58. *Not Repaired.*

BOILERS:
1213.
1499 *(new)* ?/8/13.
8431 *(new)* 20/9/30.
8215 *(ex4276)* 1/2/36.
8339 *(ex3155A)* 2/9/38.
8423 *(ex4202)* 1/5/47.
21621 22/9/50.
21630 *(ex68875)* 21/6/54.

SHEDS:
King's Cross.
Hitchin 10/1/28.
King's Cross 8/12/30.
Doncaster 29/3/45.
Retford 16/10/55.
Doncaster 23/10/55.

RENUMBERED:
4213 8/8/25.
8800 22/9/46.
68800 22/9/50.

CONDEMNED: 10/7/58.
Cut up at Doncaster.

4214

Neilson 5098.

To traffic 6/1897.

REPAIRS:
Don. ?/?—?/11/11.**G**.
Don. ?/?—?/12/16.**G**.
Don. 14/4—2/7/21.**G**.
Don. 9/6—6/9/24.**G**.
Don. 16/5—13/8/27.**G**.
Don. 15/10/29—10/1/30.**G**.
Rebuilt to J52.
Don. 5/12/31—5/3/32.**G**.
Don. 25/1—23/2/35.**G**.
Don. 26/3—30/4/38.**G**.
Don. 22/1—8/2/41.**G**.
Don. 24/2—18/3/44.**G**.
Don. 24/4—31/5/47.**G**.
Don. 2/12/50. *Not Repaired.*

BOILERS:
1214.
1212 *(ex1212)* ?/11/11.
928 *(ex928)* ?/12/16.
8351 *(new)* 10/1/30.
8654 *(ex3970)* 30/4/48.
8261 *(ex4240)* 8/2/41.

SHEDS:
King's Cross.
New England 26/4/35.
Grantham 23/1/42.

RENUMBERED:
4214 6/9/24.
8801 27/9/46.

CONDEMNED: 18/12/50.
Cut up at Doncaster.

4215

Neilson 5099.

To traffic 6/1897.

REPAIRS:
Don. ?/?—?/6/09.**G**.
Don. 20/5—3/7/20.**G**.
Don. 19/10/23—12/1/24.**G**.
Don. 15/3—5/6/26.**G**.
Don. 16/12/28—21/5/29.**G**.
Rebuilt to J52.
Don. 23/5—15/8/31.**G**.
Don. 25/10—16/11/35.**G**.
Don. 10/6—2/7/38.**G**.
Don. 7/7—4/8/41.**G**.
Don. 3—23/12/44.**G**.
Don. 6/3—21/6/48.**G**.
Str. 16/5—29/6/51.**G**.

BOILERS:
1215.
1500 *(new)* ?/6/09.
8258 *(new)* 21/5/29.
7891 *(ex4245)* 2/7/38.
8321 *(ex4248)* 4/8/41.
9638 *(new)* 21/6/48.
21734 29/6/51.

SHEDS:
King's Cross.
Hatfield 26/7/29.
King's Cross 13/11/30.
Ardsley 15/8/31.
Bradford 16/9/31.
King's Cross 18/4/35.
Hornsey 25/4/35.
King's Cross 1/4/36.

RENUMBERED:
1215N 12/1/24.
4215 12/3/25.
8802 24/10/46.
68802 19/6/48.

CONDEMNED: 27/12/54.
Into Don. for cut up 29/12/54.

3111

Doncaster 733.

To traffic 8/1897.

REPAIRS:
Don. ?/?—?/10/13.**G**.
Don. 17/7—11/11/22.**G**.
Don. 21/9/23—23/2/24.**G**.
Rebuilt to J52.
Don. 5/7—3/9/26.**G**.
Don. 31/12/27—3/3/28.**G**.
Don. 17/2—14/6/30.**G**.
Don. 6/8—12/11/32.**G**.
Don. 11/4—18/5/35.**G**.
Don. 26/10—27/11/37.**G**.
Don. 15/7—3/8/40.**G**.
Don. 28/4—27/5/44.**G**.
Str. 23/1—2/4/47.**G**.
Str. 30/5—22/7/50.**G**.
Don. 17/7/53. *Not Repaired.*

BOILERS:
111.
1755 *(ex923 & spare)* ?/10/13.
6941 *(ex1252)* 23/2/24.
8652 *(new)* 12/11/32.
8205 *(ex8808)* 2/4/47.
8262 *(ex8881)* 22/7/50.

SHEDS:
King's Cross.
Hitchin ?/?/?.
King's Cross 10/1/28.

3111 cont./
Hatfield 25/7/30.
King's Cross 12/11/30.
Hornsey 18/4/32.
King's Cross 19/11/32.

RENUMBERED:
3111 23/2/24.
8803 14/4/46.
68803 22/7/50.

CONDEMNED: 3/8/53.
Cut up at Doncaster.

3155A

Doncaster 734.

To traffic 8/1897.

REPAIRS:
Don. ?/?—?/3/05.**G**.
Don. ?/?—?/9/16.**G**.
Don. 26/4—28/6/19.**G**.
Don. 31/3—16/6/23.**G**.
Don. 28/9—26/12/25.**G**.
Rebuilt to J52.
Don. 18/5—15/11/29.**G**.
Don. 17/11—2/12/29.**N/C**.
Don. 28/12/31—8/3/32.**G**.
Don. 23/9—2/11/35.**G**.
Don. 26/6—23/7/38.**G**.
Don. 8/11—7/12/40.**G**.
Don. 27/11—22/12/43.**G**.
Don. 23/6—3/8/46.**G**.
Don. 26/3—23/4/49.**G**.
Don. 11/10—7/11/51.**G**.

BOILERS:
155.
1496 *(new)* ?/3/05.
1211 *(ex1211)* ?/9/16.
1453 *(exE1 884)* 26/12/25.
8339 *(new)* 15/11/29.
8263 *(ex3973)* 23/7/38.
8340 *(ex4270)* 3/8/46.
21634 7/11/51.

SHED:
Doncaster.

RENUMBERED:
155A ?/11/06.
3155A 26/12/25.
8804 17/11/46.
68804 23/4/49.

CONDEMNED: 17/10/55.
Into Don. for cut up 17/10/55.

The standard chimney was a plain casting and 3ft 5in. tall as here although many were altered later to a similar type but only 3ft 3in. tall as shown on No.3965 on the previous page but one.

Even with a 3ft 5in. chimney the height from rail level was 12ft 7in., the maximum permitted for engines working over the Metropolitan lines. One engine, No.964N acquired a shorter type chimney with built-up cap, which was only 2ft 10in. tall. Note load class F on the collar fitted to the vacuum standpipe, and also note the taper shank buffers.

The new company changed the painting from grey to black with single red lining, and moved the $7^1/_2$in. numbers from the bunker to the tank side, changing them to 12in. size. The first four engines changed, all in early 1923, had the ampersand in the company initials: Nos.1057 (24th February), 967 (28th February), 1058 (28th April) and 155A (16th June). In June the company initials were standardised as LNER and three got that style: 961 (29th June), 973 (28th July) and 927 (31st July).

Area suffix N was then introduced and three J53 had it put with their numbers: 925 (6th September 1923), 964 (8th November 1923) and 1215 (12th January 1924). Note the extra lamp irons to display Southern Railway lamp codes.

From the beginning of February 1924, numbers were increased by 3000, and whilst still J53 class, thirteen went direct to this from GNR grey livery: In 1924 Nos.4214 (6th September); 3975 (18th October); 3928 and 3965 (both 15th November); 3971 (29th November); 3969 (20th December): In 1925 Nos.3979 (13th February); 4055 (28th February); 4046 (4th April); 3966 (30th May); 4213 (8th August); 4211 (5th September); 3963 (21st November).

After June 1928, when red lining ceased to be applied, only five J53 came out in plain black. They were Nos.3963 (18th August 1928); 3979 (26th October 1928); 4211 (12th December 1928); 3969 (15th January 1929) all of which became J52 at their next shopping, and 3928 (8th September 1928) which remained J53 and plain black to withdrawal.

The next batch comprised ten engines which Doncaster built in 1878/9, of which only four Nos.617, 619, 620 and 633A were left to become LNER stock. Length overall was 30ft 6in. and the bunker was 6in. longer and 8in. higher to carry two tons of coal. No.620 had been rebuilt to J55 in April 1922 but No.617 was J54 to withdrawal on 24th September 1925. The other two were rebuilt to J55, No.3619 on 15th September 1927 and 633A on 16th November 1923.

Between January 1880 and August 1891, Doncaster built fifty-two more with bunkers 3ft 6in. long to give a coal capacity of 2½ tons. Only two had been scrapped by Grouping but nineteen had been rebuilt to J55 and eleven more were rebuilt by the LNER. No.808 remained a J54 to its 2nd August 1928 withdrawal but was LNER No.3808 from 13th June 1925.

(below) **Up to and including No.853, built in August 1891, only an open cab was provided and this situation was never altered. No.852 was still J54 when withdrawn 1st March 1928 as LNER 3852, having changed in February 1925 from 852N at its shed.**

CLASS J 54 & J 55

3494A

Doncaster 130.

To traffic 6/1874.

REPAIRS:
Don. ?/?—?/5/88.**G.**
Don. 18/7—27/10/23.**G.**
Rebuilt to J55.
Don. 16/8/29. *Not Repaired .*

BOILERS:
494.
494 *(new)* ?/5/88.
724 *(domeless)* 27/10/23.

SHEDS:
Bradford.
Doncaster *by* 3/25.

RENUMBERED:
N 27/10/23 *&* A *added* 29/12/23.
3494A *at shed on* 30/3/25.

CONDEMNED: 17/8/29.
Cut up at Doncaster.

3496A

Doncaster 135.

To traffic 8/1874.

REPAIRS:
Don. ?/?—?/6/90.**G.**
Don. ?/?—?/3/14.**G.**
Don. ?/?—30/9/16.**G.**
Rebuilt to J55.
Don. 23/4—18/8/23.**G.**

BOILERS:
496.
496 *(new)* ?/6/90.
804 *(ex804)* ?/3/14.
7079 *(exE1 1063)* 30/9/16.

SHEDS:
Bradford.
Doncaster *by* 5/26.

RENUMBERED:
3496A 23/2/24.

CONDEMNED: 9/6/27.
Cut up at Doncaster.

3610A

Doncaster 222.

To traffic 3/1877.

REPAIRS:
Don. ?/?—18/9/97.**G.**
Rebuilt to J55, from J56.
Don. ?/?—31/8/06.**G.**
Don. 6/10/21—4/2/22.**G.**
Don. 8/12/24—5/3/25.**G.**
Don. 17/6—3/9/27.**G.**
Don. 26/11/29. *Not Repaired.*

BOILERS:
610.
610 *(new)* 18/9/97.
1461 *(new)* 31/8/06.
1292 *(exJ4 3198)* 3/9/27.

SHED:
Lincoln.

RENUMBERED:
Duplicate **'A'** *added* 9/5/19.
3610A 5/3/25.

CONDEMNED: 27/11/29.
Cut up at Doncastser.

---

(3)617

Doncaster 255.

To traffic 12/1878.

REPAIRS:
Don. ?/?—?/11/96.**G.**
Don. 16/5—19/8/22.**G.**

BOILERS:
617.
617 *(new)* ?/11/96.

SHED:
Lincoln.

CONDEMNED: 24/9/25.
Cut up at Doncaster.

3619

Doncaster 262.

To traffic 3/1879.

REPAIRS:
Don. ?/?—?/6/04.**G.**
Don. 6/3—2/9/22.**G.**
Don. 20—30/6/23.**L.**
Don. 27/8—29/11/24.**G.**
Don. 1/4—15/9/27.**G.**
Rebuilt to J55.

BOILERS:
619.
1275 *(new)* ?/6/04.
1605 *(exE1 4070)* 15/9/27.

SHED:
Grantham.

RENUMBERED:
3619 29/11/24.

CONDEMNED: 12/4/29.
Cut up at Doncaster.

---

(3)620

Doncaster 268.

To traffic 5/1879.

REPAIRS:
Don. 7/12/21—15/4/22.**G.**
Rebuilt to J55.

BOILERS:
620.
1611 15/4/22.

SHED:
Boston.

CONDEMNED: 16/11/25.
Cut up at Doncaster.

3633A

Doncaster 276.

To traffic 9/1879.

REPAIRS:
Don. ?/?—?/10/93.**G.**
Don. 24/7—16/11/23.**G.**
Rebuilt to J55.

BOILERS:
633.
633 *(new)* ?/10/93.
743 *(4'-5" domeless)* 16/11/23.

SHED:
Bradford.

RENUMBERED:
A *added* 12/21. N *added* 16/11/23
3633A *?/2/25 at shed.*

CONDEMNED: 10/4/26.
Cut up at Doncaster.

3634A

Doncaster 280.

To traffic 1/1880.

REPAIRS:
Don. ?/?—?/10/12.**G.**
Don. 29/8—26/11/21.**G.**
Don. 15/5—18/7/25.**G.**
Don. 12/11/29. *Not Repaired.*

BOILERS:
634.
7122 *(new)* ?/10/12.

SHED:
Bradford.

RENUMBERED:
Duplicate **'A'** *added* 3/22.
3634A 18/7/25.

CONDEMNED: 15/11/29.
Cut up at Doncaster.

3635A

Doncaster 282.

To traffic 2/1880.

REPAIRS:
Don. ?/?—?/6/99.**G.**
Don. 12/5—11/8/23.**G.**
Don. 27/7/26—2/2/27.**G.**
Don. 21/11/29. *Not Repaired.*

BOILERS:
635.
635 *(new)* ?/6/99.
6903 *(ex787)* 11/8/23.

SHED:
Grantham.

RENUMBERED:
Duplicate **'A'** *added* 5/22.
3635A ?/3/25.

CONDEMNED: 23/11/29.
Cut up at Doncaster.

Beginning with No.854 built September 1891, an enclosed cab was put on, and coal rails were increased from two to three. The rest of the Doncaster order to No.860 were built similarly. No.854 became J55 in November 1914 and the LNER rebuilt No.3855 on 25th August 1927 and 3859 on 25th March 1928. But Nos.3856, 3857, 3858, 3860 remained J54 to withdrawal. Note that the number was moved from the cab to the bunker but the handrails were still of different lengths.

To the design with enclosed cab, Doncaster ordered twenty from contractors. Nos.901 to 910 came from R.Stephenson in October-December 1891, and Neilson & Co. delivered Nos.911 to 920 also during the period from October to December 1891. On these twenty the cab handrails were of equal length. All the Stephenson engines were J54 at Grouping and only three became J55 - Nos.3901, 3908, 3910, all in 1924. Five Neilson engines were already J55 at Grouping - Nos.913, 915, 916, 917 and 918, and the LNER rebuilt four more leaving only No.3914 still as J54 when withdrawn on 27th August 1931.

(below) **Six of the Doncaster built engines were on the Duplicate List with the letter A above their number from the dates shown: 139A (27th June 1906), 153A (November 1906), 633A (December 1921), 634A (March 1922), 635A (May 1922), 637A (1st July 1922).**

In 1913 Nos.804 and 858 were fitted with 4ft 2½in. diameter domeless boilers taken from withdrawn 0-6-0 tender engines. These boilers were intermediate in size between the original 4ft 0½in. pattern and Ivatt's 4ft 5in. type used for rebuilding. No.858 reverted to a 4ft 0½in. boiler in 1918. Ex works 27th July 1923, No.804 had been fitted with a further 4ft 2½in. domeless boiler which had stood spare for five years after use on GNR 0-6-0 No.649. It was (wrongly) reclassified J55 which it did not really become until it got a 4ft 5in. boiler when ex works 14th March 1931. Three others to get 4ft 2½in. boilers (with dome) in 1925/7 remained in Class J54. Note the higher pitch of the 2in. larger diameter boiler required oval instead of round windows in the cab front. The three 4ft 2½in. domed boilers from withdrawn 0-4-4 tank engines. They then kept these boilers to withdrawal: Nos.3902 (3rd April 1925 to 26th November 1930), 3906 (13th June 1925 to 3rd October 1928), 3679 (19th February 1927 to 16th January 1930).

For comparison with No.804, No.3805 with 4ft 0½in. Class J54 boiler is included. No.3805 remained J54 class until withdrawn on 23rd April 1928.

Buffers of three different types were to be seen on the class, fitted according to availability. No.3693 had parallel shank with an end collar. This was the only one to keep the Stirling pattern injector in the 1924 numbering although 675N was so fitted to withdrawal.

3636A

Doncaster 286.

To traffic 4/1880.

REPAIRS:
Don. ?/?—?/8/98.**G.**
Don. ?/?—15/12/17.**G.**
Rebuilt to J55.
Don. 21/6—28/8/20.**G.**
Don. 27/2—13/6/25.**G.**

BOILERS:
636.
636 *(new)* ?/8/98.
7387 *(new)* 15/12/17.

SHED:
Bradford.

RENUMBERED:
Duplicate '**A**' *added* 14/6/22.
3636A 13/6/25.

CONDEMNED: 2/11/28.
Cut up at Doncaster.

3637A

Doncaster 288.

To traffic 6/1880.

REPAIRS:
Don. ?/?—?/8/10.**G.**
Don. 30/4—2/9/24.**G.**
Don. 29/11/26—19/2/27.**G.**

BOILERS:
637.
6906 *(new)* ?/8/10.

SHEDS:
Doncaster.
Grantham *by* 5/26.

RENUMBERED:
Duplicate '**A**' *added* 1/7/22.
3637A 2/9/24.

CONDEMNED: 22/3/30.
Cut up at Doncaster.

3638A

Doncaster 293.

To traffic 8/1880.

REPAIRS:
Don. ?/?—28/2/08.**G.**
Rebuilt to J55.
Don. 27/2—6/9/23.**G.**
Don. 18/10/26—16/4/27.**G.**

BOILERS:
638.
61 *(exGN B7 No.61)* 28/2/08.
1171 *(exJ4 3831)* 16/4/27.

SHED:
Lincoln.

RENUMBERED:
Duplicate '**A**' *added* 8/22.
638AN 6/9/23.
3638A ?/2/25.

CONDEMNED: 24/8/29.
Cut up at Doncaster.

3153A

Doncaster 296.

To traffic 10/1880.

REPAIRS:
Don. ?/?—?/8/02.**G.**
Don. 25/8—20/11/21.**G.**
Don. 12/10/24—15/1/25.**G.**
Don. 9/8/26—10/2/27.**G.**
Rebuilt to J55.

BOILERS:
153.
1280 *(new)* ?/8/02.
7388 *(ex3803)* 10/2/27.

SHED:
Boston.

RENUMBERED:
Duplicate '**A**' *added* ?/11/06.
3153A 15/1/25.

CONDEMNED: 26/1/32.
Cut up at Doncaster.

3473A

Doncaster 305.

To traffic 12/1880.

REPAIRS:
Don. ?/?—?/3/12.**G.**
Don. ?/?—2/2/18.**G.**
Rebuilt to J55.
Don. 23/9—6/11/20.**G.**
Don. 21/12/23—3/5/24.**G.**
Don. 22/1—21/2/25.**G.**
Don. 8/1—29/3/27.**G.**

BOILERS:
473.
7118 *(new)* ?/3/12.
7384 *(new)* 2/2/18.

SHED:
King's Cross.

RENUMBERED:
Duplicate '**A**' *added* 29/10/19.
3473A 3/5/24,

CONDEMNED: 6/9/29.
Cut up at Doncaster.

3672

Doncaster 315.

To traffic 6/1881.

REPAIRS:
Don. ?/?—?/3/05.**G.**
Don. ?/?—13/5/16.**G.**
Rebuilt to J55.
Don. 26/5—17/7/20.**G.**
Don. 15/12/24—14/3/25.**G.**
Don. 8/5—4/7/25.**H.**

BOILERS:
672.
1639 *(new)* ?/3/05.
1435 *(exD4 1073)* 13/5/16.

SHED:
Colwick.

RENUMBERED:
3672 14/3/25.

CONDEMNED: 11/7/28.
Cut up at Doncaster.

3673

Doncaster 316.

To traffic 7/1881.

REPAIRS:
Don. ?/?—?/10/04.**G.**
Don. 19/9—15/12/23.**G.**
Rebuilt to J55.
Don. 18/10/26—4/6/27.**G.**

BOILERS:
673.
1642 *(new)* ?/10/04.
1090 *(exJ4 1090.domeless & spare)* 15/12/23.
1355 *(exJ4 3199.domed)* 4/6/27.

SHED:
Colwick.

RENUMBERED:
673N 15/12/23.
3673 4/6/27.

CONDEMNED: 14/5/30.
Cut up at Doncaster.

---

(3)674

Doncaster 319.

To traffic 9/1881.

REPAIRS:
Don. ?/?—?/11/96.**G.**
Don. ?/?—29/5/15.**G.**
Rebuilt to J55.
Don. 23/5—2/9/22.**G.**

BOILERS:
674.
674 *(new)* ?/11/96.
1462 *(exD4 1307)* 29/5/15.

SHED:
Colwick.

CONDEMNED: 16/11/25.
Cut up at Doncaster.

---

(3)675

Doncaster 325.

To traffic 10/1881.

REPAIRS:
Don. ?/?—?/6/02.**G.**
Don. 3/8—27/10/23.**G.**
Not rebuilt to J55.

BOILERS:
675.
1277 *(new)* ?/6/02.

SHEDS:
Hitchin.
King's Cross 25/10/26.

RENUMBERED:
675N 27/10/23.

CONDEMNED: 16/11/25.
Cut up at Doncaster.

(above) **This type of buffer with taper shank and end collar, had a solid spindle. The middle photograph on page 84 shows No.3635A still had this type to 23rd November 1929 withdrawal.**

The third buffer type had parallel shank without end collar, housing a hollow spindle. No.3789 had this type to 3rd January 1927 when it went for rebuilding to J55 class. Note it has the original sanding arrangement with a delivery point well ahead of the leading wheel.

Beginning in 1925 - No.3786 was ex works 30th May 1925 - the front sandpipes were lengthened and curved round the brake hanger to deliver the sand nearer to the wheel.

3676

Doncaster 326.

To traffic 12/1881.

REPAIRS:
Don. ?/?—?/5/12.**G.**
Don. 22/7—22/10/21.**G.**
Don. 20/7—5/9/25.**G.**

BOILERS:
676.
7121 *(new)* ?/5/12.

SHED:
King's Cross.

RENUMBERED:
3676 5/9/25.

CONDEMNED: 23/4/28.
Cut up at Doncaster.

3677

Doncaster 332.

To traffic 2/1882.

REPAIRS:
Don. ?/?—?/3/07.**G.**
Don. ?/?—30/5/14.**G.**
Rebuilt to J55.
Don. ?/?—?/3/18.**G.**
Don. 4/10/22—13/1/23.**G.**
Don. 31/8—21/11/25.**G.**
Don. 29/8—17/12/27.**G.**
Don. 7—21/12/29.**G.**

BOILERS:
677.
913 *(ex913)* ?/3/07.
1069 30/5/14.
7389 *(new)* ?/3/18.

SHED:
Bradford.

RENUMBERED:
3677 21/11/25.

CONDEMNED: 6/1/33.
Cut up at Doncaster.

3678

Doncaster 333.

To traffic 3/1882.

REPAIRS:
Don. ?/?—?/12/03.**G.**
Don. ?/?—?/8/10.**G.**
Don. ?/?—25/11/16.**G.**
Rebuilt to J55.
Don. 6/3—30/6/23.**G.**
Don. 4/8/26—13/3/27.**G.**

BOILERS:
678.
675 *(ex675)* ?/12/03.
785 *(ex785)* ?/8/10.
344 *(exJ4 1173)* 25/11/16.
1526 *(exC12 1526)* 30/6/23.

SHEDS:
Colwick.
Tuxford *by* 1/1/28.
New Holland 24/10/28.
Immingham 31/7/29.

RENUMBERED:
3678 13/3/27.

CONDEMNED: 10/8/29.
Cut up at Doncaster.

3679

Doncaster 334.

To traffic 3/1882.

REPAIRS:
Don. ?/?—?/7/04.**G.**
Don. 3/7—29/12/23.**G.**
Don. 26/8/26—19/2/27.**G.**

BOILERS:
679.
1279 *(new)* ?/7/04.
7130 *(exG1 828. 4'-2½" domed)* 19/2/27.

SHEDS:
Ardsley.
King's Cross 10/8/28.

RENUMBERED:
679N 29/12/23.
3679 19/2/27.

CONDEMNED: 16/1/30.
Cut up at Doncaster.

3680

Doncaster 335.

To traffic 5/1882.

REPAIRS:
Don. ?/?—?/10/96.**G.**
Don. ?/?—?/7/19.**G.**
Don. 18/4—28/7/23.**G.**
Don. 1/7/26—5/3/27.**G.**

BOILERS:
680.
680 *(new)* ?/10/96.
637 *(ex910)* ?/7/19.

SHEDS:
Colwick.
York 24/7/24.
Colwick ?/?/24.

RENUMBERED:
3680 5/3/27.

CONDEMNED: 14/5/30.
Cut up at Doncaster.

---

(3)681

Doncaster 340.

To traffic 9/1882.

REPAIRS:
Don. ?/?—?/2/93.**G.**
Don. ?/?—?/1/13.**G.**
Don. 21/6—21/8/20.**G.**

BOILERS:
681.
681 *(new)* ?/2/93.
688 *(ex688)* ?/1/13.

SHED:
Bradford.

CONDEMNED: 27/6/25.
Cut up at Doncaster.

3688

Doncaster 353.

To traffic 5/1883.

REPAIRS:
Don. ?/?—?/7/97.**G.**
Don. ?/?—?/5/12.**G.**
Don. 3/11/20—30/4/21.**G.**
Don. 26/12/23—12/4/24.**G.**
Rebuilt to J55.
Don. 2/8—19/10/27.**G.**

BOILERS:
688.
688 *(new)* ?/7/97.
787 *(ex787)* ?/5/12.
913 *(ex911)* 30/4/21.
1346 *(exD4 1080)* 12/4/24.

SHEDS:
Doncaster.
Colwick 12/3/28.

RENUMBERED:
3688 12/4/24.

CONDEMNED: 25/11/30.
Cut up at Doncaster.

3689

Doncaster 354.

To traffic 6/1883.

REPAIRS:
Don. ?/?—?/8/08.**G.**
Don. 12/5—21/8/20.**G.**
Don. 26/11/24—21/3/25.**G.**
Don. 9/7—22/10/27.**G.**
Rebuilt to J55.
Don. 24/1—7/2/31.**G.**

BOILERS:
689.
6899 *(new)* ?/8/08.
6881 *(exD4 4360)* 22/10/27.
8483 *(new)* 7/2/31.

SHED:
Colwick.

RENUMBERED:
3689 21/3/25.

CONDEMNED: 10/3/34.
Cut up at Doncaster.

3690

Doncaster 355.

To traffic 7/1883.

REPAIRS:
Don. ?/?—?/1/11.**G.**
Don. 6/11/23—1/3/24.**G.**
Rebuilt to J55.
Don. 15/6—25/8/27.**G.**

BOILERS:
690.
602 *(ex602)* ?/1/11.
1282 1/3/24.

SHEDS:
Colwick.
Heaton 23/7/24.
Colwick ?/?/24.

RENUMBERED:
3690 1/3/24.

CONDEMNED: 15/3/30.
Cut up at Doncaster.

No.3855 on 24th April 1926 with enclosed cab and three open coal rails on the bunker. None of the J54 class had their bunker rails plated.

At unknown dates, two engines, Nos.3903 and 3904, were fitted with a higher bunker and two footsteps were added. No.3903's bunker still had three coal rails above it.

Although No.3904's bunker was altered similarly, and had two footsteps fitted, it only had two coal rails.

The normal tall cast chimney on No.3907 was replaced by a shorter type with a separate cap but not specifically to reduce height from rail level.

(above) From 7th July 1928 No.3919 carried a shorter chimney but this was a plain cast type and without a cap.

On 22nd November 1928 No.3920 was withdrawn from Running Stock and transferred to Service Stock as yard shunter at Doncaster works.

This service locomotive had a Capital List number again from 9th April 1930 when it was renumbered 4800. On 9th August 1933 it went into works for rebuilding to J55 and Class J54 was then extinct. No.3903 withdrawn 27th April 1933 was the last in Running Stock.

The fifty-six taken over by the LNER were all grey painted with white letters and numbers. Those with open cab had the number on the cab side.

Those numbered 854 and above, with enclosed cab, had their number on the bunker. Note the $4^{1}/_{2}$in. shaded transfers on the buffer beam which were later chosen as LNER standard.

3691

Doncaster 358.

To traffic 10/1883.

REPAIRS:
Don. ?/?—?/6/02.**G.**
Don. 22/8—25/11/22.**G.**
Don. 27/9/26—5/2/27.**G.**

BOILERS:
691.
1272 *(new)* ?/6/02.

SHEDS:
Lincoln ?/1/22.
New England *at* 8/27.
Boston ?/?/?.

RENUMBERED:
3691 5/2/27.

CONDEMNED: 1/4/30.
Cut up at Doncaster.

3692

Doncaster 359.

To traffic 11/1883.

REPAIRS:
Don. ?/?—?/9/02.**G.**
Don. 6/10/22—31/1/23.**G.**
Don. 2/8/26—6/4/27.**G.**
Rebuilt to J55.

BOILERS:
692.
1278 *(new)* ?/9/02.
1155 *(exJ4 3196)* 6/4/27.

SHEDS:
Boston *still at* 8/3/24.
New England *by* 8/27.

RENUMBERED:
3692 6/4/27.

CONDEMNED: 4/2/30.
Cut up at Doncaster.

3693

Doncaster 360.

To traffic 12/1883.

REPAIRS:
Don. ?/?—?/6/98.**G.**
Don. 17/8—29/10/21.**G.**
Don. 23/10/23—15/2/24.**G.**
Gor. 21/7—15/8/25.**L.**

BOILERS:
693.
693 *(new)* ?/6/98.

SHEDS:
Trafford Park.
New England 2/1/26.

RENUMBERED:
3693 15/2/24.

CONDEMNED: 31/5/28.
Cut up at Doncaster.

3781

Doncaster 387.

To traffic 3/1885.

REPAIRS:
Don. ?/?—?/12/01.**G.**
Don. 8/11/20—12/3/21.**G.**
Don. 14/11/23—9/2/24.**G.**

BOILERS:
781.
1271 *(new)* ?/12/01.

SHEDS:
Boston.
Colwick 28/11/25.

RENUMBERED:
3781 9/2/24.

CONDEMNED: 10/4/26.
Cut up at Doncaster.

3782

Doncaster 388.

To traffic 4/1885.

REPAIRS:
Don. ?/?—?/4/99.**G.**
Don. ?/?—3/11/17.**G.**
Rebuilt to J55.
Don. 3/8—9/10/20.**G.**
Don. 8/1—21/3/25.**G.**
Don. 21/6—7/9/28.**G.**

BOILERS:
782.
782 *(new)* ?/4/99.
7381 *(new)* 3/11/17.
8142 *(new)* 7/9/28.

SHEDS:
Doncaster.
Boston 29/4/29.

RENUMBERED:
3782 21/3/25.

CONDEMNED: 28/10/31.
Cut up at Doncaster.

3783

Doncaster 399.

To traffic 11/1885.

REPAIRS:
Don. ?/?—?/10/96.**G.**
Don. ?/?—?/1/05.**G.**
Don. ?/?—15/11/19.**G.**
Rebuilt to J55.
Don. 8/12/20—26/2/21.**G.**
Don. 5/12/23—22/3/24.**G.**
Don. 1/12/27—18/2/28.**G.**
Don. 16/8—20/9/30.**G.**

BOILERS:
783.
783 *(new)* ?/10/96.
1641 *(new)* ?/1/05.
715 *(ex779)* 15/11/19.
1625 *(exJ4 3182)* 18/2/28.
8449 *(new)* 20/9/30.

SHEDS:
Doncaster.
Boston 7/3/28.
Doncaster 29/4/29.
King's Cross 25/10/33.

RENUMBERED:
3783 22/3/24.

CONDEMNED: 10/3/34.
Cut up at Doncaster.

3784

Doncaster 400.

To traffic 12/1885.

REPAIRS:
Don. ?/?—?/7/09.**G.**
Don. 1—5/2/21.**?.**
Don. 1/4—30/8/24.**G.**

BOILERS:
784.
6907 *(new)* ?/7/09.

SHED:
Doncaster.

RENUMBERED:
3784 30/8/24.

CONDEMNED: 25/10/28.
Cut up at Doncaster.

3785

Doncaster 401.

To traffic 12/1885.

REPAIRS:
Don. ?/?—?/5/09.**G.**
Don. ?/?—?/10/15.**G.**
Don. 24/11/20—9/4/21.**G.**
Don. 22/5—8/8/25.**G.**
Rebuilt to J55.
Don.7/11/27—21/1/28.**G.**

BOILERS:
785.
915 *(ex915)* ?/5/09.
674 *(ex674)* ?/10/15.
64 *(exJ4 840)* 8/8/25.
7085 *(exE1 3814)* 21/1/28.

SHED:
King's Cross.

RENUMBERED:
3785 8/8/25.

CONDEMNED: 27/10/30.
Cut up at Doncaster.

3786

Doncaster 402.

To traffic 1/1886.

REPAIRS:
Don. ?/?—?/5/09.**G.**
Don. 7/12/20—30/4/21.**G.**
Don. 6/3—30/5/25.**G.**

BOILERS:
786.
6904 *(new)* ?/5/09.

SHED:
King's Cross.

RENUMBERED:
3786 30/5/25.

CONDEMNED: 1/3/28.
Cut up at Doncaster.

In works from 6th October 1922, No.692 only went back into traffic on 31st January 1923. It was still in grey and GNR numbering but had no initials showing ownership. It kept this style to 2nd August 1926 when it went for rebuilding to J55 class.

Only one J54, No.788 ex works 17th February 1923, got L&NER and this was on black paint. In February 1925 at Boston shed its number was altered to 3788 as which it was withdrawn 10th April 1926. The next four into black with single red lining did not have the ampersand - Nos.857 (7th July), 804 (27th July), 680 (28th July), 635A (11th August), all in 1923.

(below) **During the period when the area suffix was being applied, seven J54 received such in 1923: 852N (8th September), 789N (6th October), 675N and 909N (both 27th October), 860N (17th November), 856N (22nd December) and 679N (29th December).**

From No.3781, ex works on 9th February 1924, full LNER number was put on and twenty-nine went to it directly from GNR: Nos.3153A, 3619, 3634A, 3637A, 3676, 3689, 3691, 3693, 3780, 3781, 3784, 3786, 3801, 3805, 3808, 3853, 3855, 3858, 3859, 3902 to 3907, 3911, 3914, 3919, 3920. The last in GNR was No.691, ex works 25th November 1922 which went to works next on 27th September 1926 but was only out as 3691 on 5th February 1927.

(above) **Those on the Duplicate List duly got 3xxx numbers with the 'A' at the end and not above as had been GNR custom.**

Subsequent to the abolishment of red lining in June 1928, only four J54 had repaints which put them into plain black. These were Nos.3853 (7th September 1928), 3858 (12th October 1928), 3860 (13th April 1929) and 3801 (17th August 1929). The last of the class, No.3903 just managed to retain lining being ex works on 26th May 1928.

3787

Doncaster 403.

To traffic 2/1886.

REPAIRS:
Don. ?/?—?/11/96.**G**.
Don. ?/?—?/9/10.**G**.
Don. 1/2—8/4/22.**G**.
Rebuilt to J55.
Don. 18/2—24/5/24.**G**.

BOILERS:
787.
787 *(new)* ?/11/96.
6903 *(new)* ?/9/10.
1291 8/4/22.

SHED:
Doncaster.

RENUMBERED:
3787 24/5/24.

CONDEMNED: 22/11/28.
Cut up at Doncaster.

3788

Doncaster 404.

To traffic 3/1886.

REPAIRS:
Don. ?/?—?/11/12.**G**.
Don. 1/11/22—17/2/23.**G**.

BOILERS:
788.
7123 *(new)* ?/11/12.

SHED:
Boston.

RENUMBERED:
3788 ?/2/25.

CONDEMNED: 10/4/26.
Cut up at Doncaster.

3789

Doncaster 429.

To traffic 12/1886.

REPAIRS:
Don. ?/?—?/1/05.**G**.
Don. 26/3—29/5/20.**G**.
Don. 4/6—6/10/23.**G**.
Don. 3/1—12/3/27.**G**.
Rebuilt to J55.

BOILERS:
789.
1640 *(new)* ?/1/05.
1130 *(exJ4 3832)* 12/3/27.

SHEDS:
New England.
Colwick 30/11/25.

RENUMBERED:
789N 6/10/23.
3789 12/3/27.

CONDEMNED: 30/4/30.
Cut up at Doncaster.

3790

Doncaster 430.

To traffic 1/1887.

REPAIRS:
Don. ?/?—?/4/89.**G**.
Don. ?/?—7/3/14.**G**.
Rebuilt to J55.
Don. ?/?—?/3/18.**G**.
Don. 22/7—15/10/21.**G**.
Don. 5/12/24—14/2/25.**G**.
Don. 16/2—23/3/29.**G**.
Don. 29/4—20/5/33.**G**.

BOILERS:
790.
790 *(new)* ?/4/89.
1072 *(exD4 1319)* 7/3/14.
7385 *(new)* ?/3/18.
8160 *(new)* 23/3/29.

SHEDS:
Boston.
Doncaster ?/?/?.

RENUMBERED:
3790 14/2/25.

CONDEMNED: 22/9/36.
Cut up at Doncaster.

3779

Doncaster 439.

To traffic 6/1887.

REPAIRS:
Don. ?/?—16/11/12.**G**.
Rebuilt to J55.
Don. ?/?—?/3/18.**G**.
Don. 24/11/19—14/2/20.**G**.
Don. 16/7—20/9/24.**G**.
Don. 1/12/26—17/3/27.**G**.

BOILERS:
779.
715 *(exE1 715)* 16/11/12.
7390 *(new)* ?/3/18.

SHEDS:
Doncaster.
Boston 9/3/28.
Grantham 1/4/30.

RENUMBERED:
3779 20/9/24.

CONDEMNED: 28/4/30.
Cut up at Doncaster.

3780

Doncaster 440.

To traffic 6/1887.

REPAIRS:
Don. ?/?—?/8/13.**G**.
Don. 22/11/20—2/4/21.**G**.
Don. 24/9/24—3/1/25.**G**.

BOILERS:
780.
7119 *(new)* ?/8/13.

SHED:
Doncaster.

RENUMBERED:
3780 3/1/25.

CONDEMNED: 14/6/29.
Cut up at Doncaster.

3801

Doncaster 453.

To traffic 2/1888.

REPAIRS:
Don. ?/?—?/3/12.**G**.
Don. 17/8—5/11/21.**G**.
Don. 8/9/24—7/2/25.**G**.
Don. 20/7—17/8/29.**G**.

BOILERS:
801.
7117 *(new)* ?/3/12.

SHED:
Doncaster.

RENUMBERED:
3801 7/2/25.

CONDEMNED: 17/10/32.
Cut up at Doncaster.

3802

Doncaster 454.

To traffic 3/1888.

REPAIRS:
Don. ?/?—10/8/12.**G**.
Rebuilt to J55.
Don. ?/?—?/4/16.**G**.
Don. 10/8—29/10/21.**G**.
Don. 12/5—11/7/25.**G**.
Don. 17/9—12/10/28.**G**.
Don. 29/8—19/9/31.**G**.
Don. 2—9/4/32.**L**.

BOILERS:
802.
894 *(exE1 894)* 10/8/12.
362 *(exJ4 375)* ?/4/16.
8514 *(new)* 19/9/31.

SHEDS:
Bradford *at* 1/22.
King's Cross 30/12/22.

RENUMBERED:
3802 11/7/25.

CONDEMNED: 19/7/34.
Cut up at Doncaster.

3803

Doncaster 459.

To traffic 4/1888.

REPAIRS:
Don. ?/?—?/4/00.**G**.
Don. ?/?—22/5/15.**G**.
Rebuilt to J55.
Don. ?/?—?/12/17.**G**.
Don. 12—26/4/19.**L**.
Don. 16/7—11/10/24.**G**.

BOILERS:
803.
803 *(new)* ?/4/00.
1432 22/5/15.
7388 *(new)* ?/12/17.

SHED:
Doncaster.

RENUMBERED:
3803 11/10/24.

CONDEMNED: 7/8/26.
Cut up at Doncaster.

From the J54 series built in 1874, which were 29ft 6in. overall and had only 2ft 6in. long bunkers, two became J55, No.496 on 30th September 1916 and No.494 on 27th October 1923. Both were made 'A' stock later, No.494 on 29th December 1923 and No.3496A on 23rd February 1924. As J55 they were not alike as 494 (*see* opposite, bottom and page 102, bottom) got a domeless 4ft 5in. boiler with Stirling safety valve cover, but 496 had a domed boiler with an Ivatt cover. No.494 also had normal rear sanding fitted and 3496A kept the original arrangement of a box on the running plate, feeding to the rear of the middle wheels.

(above) **At Grouping, in J55 class, there were twenty-two engines which had open cab and with their number on the side of the cab. All were in grey paint and unlined**

After the LNER took over, a further fourteen of the open cab type were rebuilt with 4ft 5in. boiler, No.3804 being the last, ex works 14th March 1931.

At Grouping there were six J55 - Nos.854, 913, 915, 916, 917 and 918 - which had enclosed cab and higher bunker. The LNER rebuilt nine more, eight of these were Running Stock - Nos.3855, 3859, 3901, 3908, 3910, 3911, 3912, and 3919 which was the last being ex works 7th March 1931. Finally No.4800 (ex3920) in Service Stock became J55 from 9th September 1933.

Between 27th October 1923 and 2nd February 1924, the LNER used four domeless 4ft 5in. boilers to rebuild Nos.494, 633A, 673 and 912 to J55, three of these having stood spare since the end of 1916. Nos.3494A, 3633A and 3912 kept their domeless boilers to withdrawal but, ex works 4th June 1927, No.3673 had changed to a domed type.

3804

Doncaster 468.

To traffic 8/1888.

REPAIRS:
Don. ?/?—?/4/13.**G**.
Don. 28/4—27/7/23.**G**.
Reclassified J55.
Don. 18/10/26—27/1/27.**G**.
Don. 28/2—14/3/31.**G**.
Rebuilt to J55 Standard.

BOILERS:
804.
484 *(ex 0-6-0 484: 10'-0" barrel:4'-2½" dia. domeless)* ?/4/13.
649 *(ex 0-6-0 649: 10'-1" barrel:4'-2½" dia. domeless)* 27/7/23.
8488 *(new)* 14/3/31.

SHEDS:
Bradford.
Hornsey *by* 1/9/23.
King's Cross 13/1/30.

RENUMBERED:
3804 4/3/25.

CONDEMNED: 30/9/33.
Cut up at Doncaster.

3805

Doncaster 481.

To traffic 4/1889.

REPAIRS:
Don. ?/?—?/12/96.**G**.
Don. ?/?—?/10/10.**G**.
Don. 17/2—23/4/21.**G**.
Don. 25/6—18/10/24.**G**.
Don. 26/5—13/8/27.**G**.

BOILERS:
805.
805 *(new)* ?/12/96.
6902 *(new)* ?/10/10.

SHEDS:
Bradford.
King's Cross *by* 12/3/23.

RENUMBERED:
3805 18/10/24.

CONDEMNED: 23/4/28.
Cut up at Doncaster.

3806

Doncaster 482.

To traffic 5/1889.

REPAIRS:
Don. ?/?—17/11/17.**G**.
Rebuilt to J55.
Don. 21/9—13/11/20.**G**.
Don. 15/12/24—5/3/25.**G**.
Don. 1/11/27—21/3/28.**G**.

BOILERS:
806.
7382 *(new)* 17/11/17.
7824 21/3/28.

SHEDS:
Copley Hill.
King's Cross *by* 6/5/24.
Hatfield 17/4/28.

RENUMBERED:
3806 5/3/25.

CONDEMNED: 26/6/30.
Cut up at Doncaster.

3397

Doncaster 509.

To traffic 5/1890.

REPAIRS:
Don. ?/?—13/12/13.**G**.*Reb. J55.*
Don. 18/6—7/9/23.**G**.
Don. 10/10—19/12/27.**G**.

BOILERS:
397.
1162 *(exJ4 1126)* 13/12/13.

SHED:
Bradford.

RENUMBERED:
397N 7/9/23.
3397 19/12/27.

CONDEMNED: 14/1/30.
Cut up at Doncaster.

3139A

Doncaster 511.

To traffic 7/1890.

REPAIRS:
Don. ?/?—?/9/16.**G**.
Don. 20/5—20/8/21.**G**.
Don. 16/11/23—8/3/24.**G**.
Rebuilt to J55.
Don. 25/8—12/11/27.**G**.

BOILERS:
139.
903 *(ex903)* ?/9/16.
1424 *(exJ4 1140)* 8/3/24.
1463 *(exC12 4010)* 12/11/27.

SHEDS:
King's Cross.
Hornsey *by* 6/5/24.

RENUMBERED:
139A 27/6/06.
3139A 8/3/24.

CONDEMNED: 9/1/30.
Cut up at Doncaster.

3807

Doncaster 521.

To traffic 11/1890.

REPAIRS:
Don. ?/?—?/8/14.**G**.
Don. 25/7—2/12/22.**G**.
Don. 15/8—21/11/25.**G**.
Rebuilt to J55.
Don. 7/9—11/10/28.**G**.
Don. 6—20/6/31.**G**.

BOILERS:
807.
790 *(ex790)* ?/8/14.
1472 *(exC12 4531)* 21/11/25.
8151 *(new)* 11/10/28.

SHEDS:
Doncaster.
Hatfield *after* 6/25.
King's Cross 7/3/28.

RENUMBERED:
3807 21/11/25.

CONDEMNED: 13/10/33.
Cut up at Doncaster.

3808

Doncaster 523.

To traffic 1/1891.

REPAIRS:
Don. ?/?—?/12/96.**G**.
Don. ?/?—?/2/05.**G**.
Don. 22/11/20—26/3/21.**G**.
Don. 24/3—13/6/25.**G**.
Don. 14/9—20/11/26.**G**.

BOILERS:
808.
808 *(new)* ?/12/96.
1638 *(new)* ?/2/05.

SHEDS:
Bradford.
King's Cross 30/12/22.

RENUMBERED:
3808 13/6/25.

CONDEMNED: 2/8/28.
Cut up at Doncaster.

3809

Doncaster 527.

To traffic 3/1891.

REPAIRS:
Don. ?/?—3/10/14.**G**.*Reb.J55.*
Don. 24/11/20—26/3/21.**G**.
Don. 23/8—8/11/23.**G**.
Don. 3/11/26—8/1/27.**G**.

BOILERS:
809.
1156 *(exJ4 1156)* 3/10/14.

SHEDS:
Bradford.
Lincoln ?/?/?.

RENUMBERED:
809N 8/11/23.
3809 8/1/27.

CONDEMNED: 16/3/29.
Cut up at Lincoln.

3810

Doncaster 530.

To traffic 4/1891.

REPAIRS:
Don. ?/?—4/4/14.**G**.
Rebuilt to J55.
Don. 10/11/21—11/2/22.**G**.
Don. 12/10/25—8/1/26.**G**.

BOILERS:
810.
396 *(exJ4 334)* 4/4/14.

SHEDS:
Copley Hill.
Lincoln ?/?/?.

RENUMBERED:
3810 8/1/26.

CONDEMNED: 27/8/28.
Cut up at Doncaster.

3851

Doncaster 536.

To traffic 5/1891.

REPAIRS:
Don. ?/?—?/7/10.**G**.
Don. ?/?—28/10/16.**G**.
Rebuilt to J55.
Don. 6/11/23—16/2/24.**G**.
Don. 3/1—30/4/27.**G**.
Don. 17/5—14/6/30.**G**.

BOILERS:
851.
495 *(ex495)* ?/7/10.
1307 *(exJ4 1127)* 28/10/16.
1069 *(ex677)* 16/2/24.
7080 *(exJ4 4149)* 30/4/27.

SHED:
Colwick.

RENUMBERED:
3851 16/2/24.

CONDEMNED: 30/9/33.
Cut up at Doncaster.

3852

Doncaster 538.

To traffic 6/1891.

REPAIRS:
Don. 16/11/20—19/3/21.**G**.
Don. 9/7—8/9/23.**H**.
Don. 26/12/23—2/2/24.**G**.

BOILERS:
852.
1276 8/9/23.

SHED:
Doncaster.

RENUMBERED:
852N 2/2/24.
3852 at shed 2/25.

CONDEMNED: 1/3/28.
Cut up at Doncaster.

3853

Doncaster 544.

To traffic 8/1891.

REPAIRS:
Don. ?/?—?/4/14.**G**.
Don. 9/10/22—6/1/23.**G**.
Don. 23/11/25—6/2/26.**G**.
Don. 7/8—7/9/28.**G**.

BOILERS:
853.
7125 *(new)* ?/4/14.

SHED:
Bradford.

RENUMBERED:
3853 6/2/26.

CONDEMNED: 3/8/32.
Cut up at Doncaster.

3854

Doncaster 548.

To traffic 9/1891.

REPAIRS:
Don. ?/?—7/11/14.**G**.
Rebuilt to J55.
Don. 29/11/20—26/3/21.**G**.
Don. 23/1—28/3/25.**G**.

BOILERS:
854.
1607 7/11/14.

SHED:
Bradford.

RENUMBERED:
3854 28/3/25.

CONDEMNED: 10/11/28.
Cut up at Doncaster.

3855

Doncaster 551.

To traffic 10/1891.

REPAIRS:
Don. ?/?—?/11/09.**G**.
Don. 8/5—26/11/21.**G**.
Don. 19/8—13/12/24.**G**.
Don. 8/6—25/8/27.**G**.
Rebuilt to J55.

BOILERS:
855.
6905 *(new)* ?/11/09.
1274 26/11/21.
1752 *(exJ4 3195)* 25/8/27.

SHEDS:
Hatfield 30/9/22.
King's Cross 7/7/23.

RENUMBERED:
3855 13/12/24.

CONDEMNED: 18/2/30.
Cut up at Doncaster.

3856

Doncaster 555.

To traffic 11/1891.

REPAIRS:
Don. ?/?—?/1/17.**G**.
Don. 25/9—22/12/23.**G**.
Don. 12/6—2/9/27.**G**.

BOILERS:
856.
1639 *(ex672)* ?/1/17.

SHEDS:
Boston.
Grantham 28/5/29.

RENUMBERED:
856N 22/12/23.
3856 2/9/27.

CONDEMNED: 5/3/30.
Cut up at Doncaster.

3857

Doncaster 559.

To traffic 12/1891.

REPAIRS:
Don. ?/?—?/8/11.**G**.
Don. 8/3—7/7/23.**G**.
Don. 16/11/25—13/2/26.**G**.

BOILERS:
857.
6995 *(new)* ?/8/11.

SHED:
King's Cross.

RENUMBERED:
3857 21/2/25.

CONDEMNED: 10/10/28.
Cut up at Doncaster.

3858

Doncaster 564.

To traffic 2/1892.

REPAIRS:
Don. ?/?—?/12/97.**G**.
Don. ?/?—?/5/13.**G**.
Don. ?/?—?/6/18.**G**.
Don. 5/7—21/8/20.**G**.
Don. 18/5—25/7/25.**G**.
Don. 18/9—12/10/28.**G**.

BOILERS:
858.
858 *(new)* ?/12/97.
435 *(ex 0-6-0 481;10'-0" barrel:4'-2$^{1}/_{2}$" dia. domeless)* ?/5/13.
7118 *(ex3473)* ?/6/18.

SHEDS:
Copley Hill.
Ardsley ?/?/?.
Copley Hill 30/4/30.
Ardsley 30/6/30.

RENUMBERED:
3858 25/7/25.

CONDEMNED: 12/7/32.
Cut up at Doncaster.

3859

Doncaster 568.

To traffic 3/1892.

REPAIRS:
Don. ?/?—?/6/98.**G**.
Don. ?/?—?/7/08.**G**.
Don. 27/9/22—13/1/23.**G**.
Don. 16/2—9/5/25.**G**.
Don. 17/11/27—25/3/28.**G**.
Rebuilt to J55.
Don. 18/6—27/8/32.**G**.
Don. 30/11—29/12/34.**G**.
Don. 30/12/38--28/1/39.**G**.
Don. 18/12/42—9/1/43.**G**.

WORKS CODES:- Cow - Cowlairs. Dar - Darlington. Don - Doncaster. Ghd - Gateshead. Gor - Gorton. Inv - Inverurie. Kit - Kittybrewster. RSH - Robert, Stephenson & Hawthorn. Str - Stratford. Yk - York.
REPAIR CODES:- **C/H** - Casual Heavy. **C/L** - Casual Light. **G** - General. **H**- Heavy. **H/I** - Heavy Intermediate. **L** - Light. **L/I** - Light Intermediate. **N/C** - Non-Classified.

Until 1928 all J55 boilers had Ramsbottom safety valves and those with a dome had the Ivatt type cast iron enclosure, only the four domeless boilers having the Stirling design of brass trumpet, having been built April 1896 to July 1898.

Beginning with No.3908 ex works 31st March 1928, and No.3911 out 19th May 1928, newly built boilers were put on J55 class and these were fitted with Ross 'pop' safety valves.

The chimney usually fitted was the built-up type but some kept the 3ft 3in. single piece casting, more often associated with those on J54 class. Apart from No.3690 - fitted 1st March 1924 - only those J55 with domeless boiler had this type.

This was the normal style of chimney carried by J55 class with height from rail of 12ft 7in. against the 13ft 0in. of the plain casting type. There was one subsequent change, from 1940 a 2in. shorter chimney was fitted to the three survivors, as shown by the bottom three photographs on page 103.

3859 cont./
Don. 3/12/45—12/1/46.**G.**

BOILERS:
859.
859 *(new)* ?/6/98.
6898 *(new)* ?/7/08.
7382 *(ex3806)* 25/3/28.
8310 *(ex3901)* 29/12/34.

SHEDS:
Copley Hill.
Ardsley 12/11/30.
Copley Hill 2/1/31.
Ardsley 19/2/32.
Copley Hill 19/9/32.
Ardsley 1/12/32.
Bradford 31/5/33.
New England 10/2/44.
Doncaster 23/9/45.

RENUMBERED:
3859 9/5/25.
8317 17/6/46.

CONDEMNED: 24/12/48.
Cut up at Doncaster.

3860

Doncaster 570.

To traffic 4/1892.

REPAIRS:
Don. ?/?—?/8/00.**G.**
Don. 2/10—17/11/23.**G.**
Don. 16/6—1/9/26.**G.**
Don. 16/3—13/4/29.**G.**

BOILERS:
860.
860 *(new)* ?/8/00.
7123 *(ex3788)* 1/9/26.

SHEDS:
Copley Hill.
Ardsley 9/1/28.
King's Cross 10/8/28.

RENUMBERED:
860N 17/11/23.
3860 1/9/26.

CONDEMNED: 1/8/31.
Cut up at Doncaster.

3901

R. Stephenson & Co. 2751.

To traffic 10/1891.

REPAIRS:
Don. ?/?—?/12/10.**G.**
Don. 20/10—11/12/20.**G.**
Don. 20/2—28/6/24.**G.**
Rebuilt to J55.
Don. 4/4—11/6/27.**G.**
Don. 28/9—19/10/29.**G.**
Don. 6—27/2/32.**G.**

BOILERS:
901.
805 *(ex805)* ?/12/10.
1508 *(exC12 1548)* 28/6/24.
8310 *(new)* 19/10/29.

SHEDS:
Hatfield.
King's Cross 6/1/23.

RENUMBERED:
3901 28/6/24.

CONDEMNED: 29/9/34.
Cut up at Doncaster.

3902

R. Stephenson & Co. 2752.

To traffic 10/1891.

REPAIRS:
Don. ?/?—?/10/13.**G.**
Don. 10/5—2/9/22.**G.**
Don. 15/12/24—3/4/25.**G.**
Don. 16/1—15/3/28.**G.**

BOILERS:
902.
858 *(ex858)* ?/10/13.
1532 *(exG1 932; 4'-2½"; domed)* 3/4/25.

SHEDS:
Copley Hill.
Ardsley ?/?/?.

RENUMBERED:
3902 3/4/25.

CONDEMNED: 26/11/30.
Cut up at Doncaster.

3903

R. Stephenson & Co. 2753.

To traffic 11/1891.

REPAIRS:
Don. ?/?—?/6/15.**G.**
Don. 5/10—20/11/20.**G.**
Don. 5/2—4/4/25.**G.**
Don. 1/4—26/5/28.**G.**

BOILERS:
903.
7126 *(new)* ?/6/15.

SHED:
Bradford.

RENUMBERED:
3903 4/4/25.

CONDEMNED: 27/4/33.
Cut up at Doncaster.

3904

R. Stephenson & Co. 2754.

To traffic 11/1891.

REPAIRS:
Don. ?/?—?/12/15.**G.**
Don. 22/3—18/6/21.**G.**
Don. 5/5—30/8/24.**G.**
Don. 15/1—5/3/27.**G.**

BOILERS:
904.
803 *(ex803)* ?/12/15.

SHED:
Bradford.

RENUMBERED:
3904 30/8/24.

CONDEMNED: 13/5/30.
Cut up at Doncaster.

3905

R. Stephenson & Co. 2755.

To traffic 12/1891.

REPAIRS:
Don. ?/?—?/2/13.**G.**
Don. 28/9—13/11/20.**G.**
Don. 8/1—5/4/24.**G.**
Don. 14/7—16/9/26.**G.**
Don. 31/8—5/10/29.**G.**

BOILERS:
905.
7124 *(new)* ?/2/13.

SHEDS:
Grantham.
Boston 1/1/32.
Grantham 5/3/32.

RENUMBERED:
3905 5/4/24.

CONDEMNED: 30/12/32.
Cut up at Doncaster.

3906

R. Stephenson & Co. 2756.

To traffic 12/1891.

REPAIRS:
Don. ?/?—?/10/13.**G.**
Don. 30/3—13/8/21.**G.**
Don. 31/3—13/6/25.**G.**

BOILERS:
906.
905 *(ex905)* ?/10/13.
787 *(ex688)* 13/8/21.
6911 *(ex G1 824: 4'-2½"; domed)* 13/6/25.

SHED:
Colwick.

RENUMBERED:
3906 13/6/25.

CONDEMNED: 3/10/28.
Cut up at Doncaster.

3907

R. Stephenson & Co. 2757.

To traffic 12/1891.

REPAIRS:
Don. ?/?—?/10/08.**G.**
Don. 15/10—4/12/20.**G.**
Don. 4/12/24—26/2/25.**G.**
Don. 15/2—13/4/28.**G.**

BOILERS:
907.
6900 *(new)* ?/10/08.

SHEDS:
Boston.
New England 14/3/31.

RENUMBERED:
3907 26/2/25.

CONDEMNED: 29/12/31.
Cut up at Doncaster.

(above) **When No.3919 became J55, ex works 7th March 1931, it had a new boiler on which a modern type of injector was used, fitted below the tank instead of on the firebox backplate. Only Nos.3689 (7th February 1931), 3804 (14th March 1931) and 3802 (19th September 1931) were also fitted with this type of injector.**

Until 1931 all coal rails were open type on both types of cab and whether two, or three were fitted.

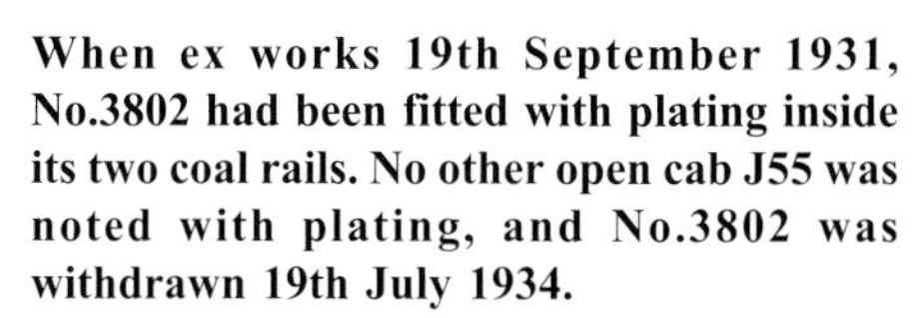

When ex works 19th September 1931, No.3802 had been fitted with plating inside its two coal rails. No other open cab J55 was noted with plating, and No.3802 was withdrawn 19th July 1934.

(above) **At the end of 1934 there were only five J55 left and only No.3790 was an open cab type. Although coal rails were fitted in the 1890s, odd ones never got them and two J55 never had them. These were Nos.3790 and 3153A withdrawn 22nd September 1936 and 26th January 1932 respectively.**

The other four then had plating put inside their rails, all being three rail types - 3918 (6th October 1934), 3859 (29th December 1934), 3908 (28th September 1935), 4800 (25th April 1936).

There were two whistle positions without any clear pattern. No.3473A was one which had it above the cab roof.

3908

R. Stephenson & Co. 2758.

To traffic 12/1891.

REPAIRS:
Don. ?/?—?/8/05.**G.**
Don. 13/10/21—18/2/22.**G.**
Don. 6/8—31/10/24.**G.**
Rebuilt to J55.
Don. 18/11/27—31/3/28.**G.**
Don. 9/3—1/6/31.**G.**
Don. 23/8—28/9/35.**G.**
Don. 2/3—23/4/38.**G.**
Don. 28/1—22/2/41.**G.**
Don. 20/2—18/3/44.**G.**
Don. 12/5/47. *Not Repaired*

BOILERS:
908.
808 *(ex808)* ?/8/05.
1524 *(exC12 4529)* 31/10/24.
8064 *(new)* 31/3/28.
8319 *(exC12 4510)* 23/4/38.

SHEDS:
Lincoln.
Ardsley 2/3/29.
Bradford 5/3/29.
King's Cross 21/8/34.
New England 5/7/43.
Doncaster 23/9/45.

RENUMBERED:
3908 31/10/24.
8318 26/5/46.

CONDEMNED: 27/5/47.
Cut up at Doncaster.

3909

R. Stephenson & Co. 2759.

To traffic 12/1891.

REPAIRS:
Don. ?/?—?/10/08.**G.**
Don. 26/1—20/3/20.**G.**
Don. 23/8—27/10/23.**G.**
Don. 1/12/25—20/2/26.**G.**

BOILERS:
909.
6901 *(new)* ?/10/08.

SHEDS:
Hatfield.
King's Cross 17/4/28.

RENUMBERED:
909N 27/10/23.
3909 20/2/26.

CONDEMNED: 27/6/28.
Cut up at Doncaster.

3910

R. Stephenson & Co. 2760.

To traffic 12/1891.

REPAIRS:
Don. ?/?—?/1/11.**G.**
Don. ?/?—?/6/19.**G.**
Don. 1/7—9/9/22.**G.**
Don. 17/4—30/8/24.**G.**
Rebuilt to J55.
Don. 27/9—18/12/26.**G.**
Don. 5/10—7/11/28.**G.**

BOILERS:
910.
637 *(ex637)* ?/1/11.
498 *(ex498)* ?/6/19.
6815 *(exE1 995)* 30/8/24.
1151 *(exJ4 3718)* 18/12/26.

SHEDS:
King's Cross.
Hitchin 25/10/24.

RENUMBERED:
3910 30/8/24.

CONDEMNED: 1/8/31.
Cut up at Doncaster.

3911

Neilson 4398.

To traffic 10/1891.

REPAIRS:
Don. ?/?—?/6/15.**G.**
Don. 6/10—27/11/20.**G.**
Don. 8/1—21/3/25.**G.**
Don. 27/2—19/5/28.**G.**
Rebuilt to J55.
Don. 15/8—5/9/31.**G.**

BOILERS:
911.
913 *(ex677)* ?/6/15.
1641 *(ex783)* 27/11/20.
8063 *(new)* 19/5/28.

SHEDS:
Doncaster.
New England 1/6/28.
King's Cross 1/9/31.

RENUMBERED:
3911 21/3/25.

CONDEMNED: 10/3/34.
Cut up at Doncaster.

3912

Neilson 4399.

To traffic 10/1891.

REPAIRS:
Don. 5/4—9/8/19.**G.**
Don. 25/10/23—2/2/24.**G.**
Rebuilt to J55.
Don. 14/2—9/4/27.**G.**

BOILERS:
912.
782 *(ex782)* 9/8/19.
1030 *(exJ7 1021 & spare:domeless)* 2/2/24.

SHED:
Bradford.

RENUMBERED:
912N 2/2/24.
3912 9/4/27.

CONDEMNED: 4/12/30.
Cut up at Doncaster.

3913

Neilson 4400.

To traffic 11/1891.

REPAIRS:
Don. ?/?—30/3/06.**G.**
Rebuilt to J55.
Don. 5/11—24/12/19.**G.**
Don. 2/9—24/12/24.**G.**
Don. 19/1—4/5/28.**G.**

BOILERS:
913.
606 *(ex606)* 30/3/06.
1072 *(ex790)* 24/12/19.
381 *(exJ4 315)* 24/12/24.

SHEDS:
Bradford.
Ardsley *by* 1/28.

RENUMBERED:
3913 24/12/24.

CONDEMNED: 25/11/31.
Cut up at Doncaster.

3914

Neilson 4401.

To traffic 11/1891.

REPAIRS:
Don. ?/?—?/6/11.**G.**
Don. 7/7—18/9/20.**G.**
Don. 28/2—4/7/24.**G.**
Don. 22/6—1/9/27.**G.**

BOILERS:
914.
6997 *(new)* ?/6/11.

SHED:
Bradford.

RENUMBERED:
3914 4/7/24.

CONDEMNED: 27/8/31.
Cut up at Doncaster.

3915

Neilson 4402.

To traffic 11/1891.

REPAIRS:
Don. ?/?—?/12/08.**G.**
Don. ?/?—25/11/16.**G.**
Rebuilt to J55.
Don. 23/6—7/10/22.**G.**
Don. 23/10/25—23/1/26.**G.**
Don. 17/10—17/12/27.**G.**
Don. 30/8—4/10/30.**G.**

BOILERS:
915.
907 *(ex907)* ?/12/08.
6962 25/11/16.
6959 *(exJ7 3188)* 17/12/27.

SHEDS:
Copley Hill.
Ardsley *by* 6/27.

RENUMBERED:
3915 23/1/26.

CONDEMNED: 15/2/33.
Cut up at Doncaster.

The other position was on the front plate of the cab, high as on No.3689 or low as on No.3918 (*see* bottom illustration).

(below) **A few of the contractor built engines, Nos.3901 to 3920 with the higher bunker, had two footsteps added on the bunker side.**

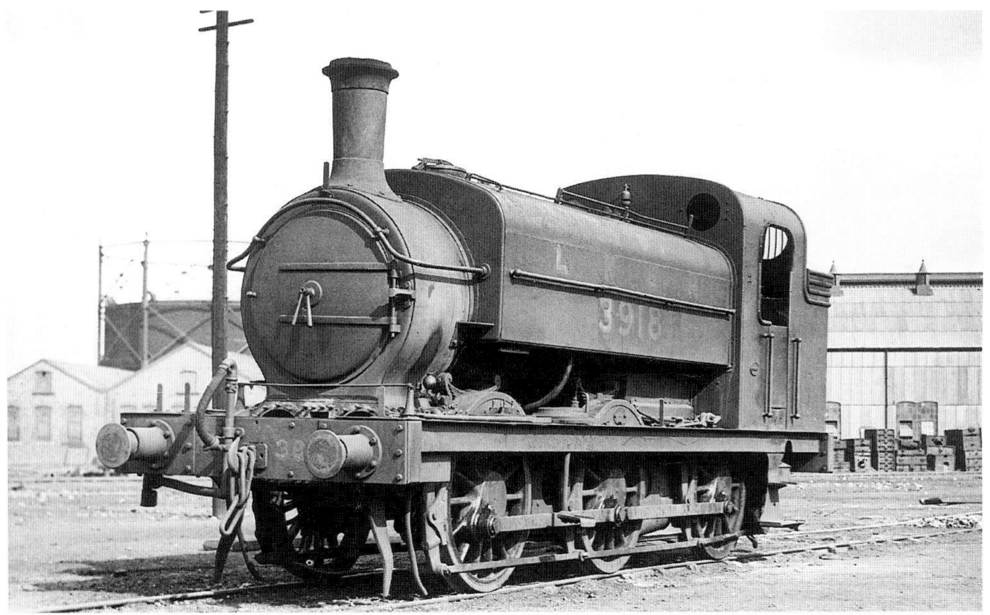

By no means did all of the last twenty built get steps on the bunker - compare with the middle photograph on page 102 of No.916 which got them on both sides.

Three buffer types could be seen on the class, but this short taper shank type with hollow spindle appears only on Nos.3473A and 3494A.

(below) **Most had this parallel shank type without end collar and with a hollow spindle. Note load class 3 collar on the standpipe.**

The remainder had the longer taper-shank type with an end collar and solid spindle. Only No.3783 was fitted with Westinghouse brake equipment, and this was for testing dual fitted East Coast Joint Stock coaches. The engine brake was vacuum as on all the others.

3916

Neilson 4403.

To traffic 11/1891.

REPAIRS:
Don. ?/?—2/8/13.**G**.
Rebuilt to J55.
Don. 29/10—17/12/21.**G**.
Don. 30/10/22—10/2/23.**G**.
Don. 9/12/26—26/3/27.**G**.

BOILERS:
916.
1140 *(exJ4 1122)* 2/8/13.

SHED:
Bradford.

RENUMBERED:
3916 26/3/27.

CONDEMNED: 1/8/31.
Cut up at Doncaster.

3917

Neilson 4404.

To traffic 11/1891.

REPAIRS:
Don. ?/?—?/5/10.**G**.
Don. 23/5—9/9/22.**G**.
Rebuilt to J55.
Don. 12/10—19/12/25.**G**.
Don. 16/7—23/9/27.**G**.

BOILERS:
917.
909 *(ex909)* ?/5/10.
192 9/9/22.
6839 *(exC12 4541)* 23/9/27.

SHED:
Colwick.

RENUMBERED:
3917 19/12/25.

CONDEMNED: 23/6/30.
Cut up at Doncaster.

3918

Neilson 4405.

To traffic 12/1891.

REPAIRS:
Don. ?/?—14/6/07.**G**.
Rebuilt to J55.
Don. 18/2—10/4/20.**G**.
Don. 4/4—16/6/23.**G**.
Don. 9/12/25—27/2/26.**G**.
Don. 30/8—29/9/28.**G**.
Don. 15/8—19/9/31.**G**.
Don. 29/9—6/10/34.**G**.

BOILERS:
918.
610 *(ex 610)* 14/6/07.
1432 10/4/20.
1062 16/6/23.
1462 *(ex674)* 27/2/26.
8149 *(new)* 29/9/28.
8063 *(ex3911)* 6/10/34.

SHEDS:
Colwick.
York 8/8/24.
Colwick ?/?/24.

RENUMBERED:
3918 27/2/26.

CONDEMNED: 11/3/37.
Cut up at Doncaster.

3919

Neilson 4406.

To traffic 12/1891.

REPAIRS:
Don. ?/?—?/3/11.**G**.
Don. 22/4—13/8/21.**G**.
Don. 23/10/24—3/4/25.**G**.
Don. 31/5—7/7/28.**G**.
Don. 21/2—7/3/31.**G**.
Rebuilt to J55.
Don. 12—26/5/34.**G**.

BOILERS:
919.
6999 *(new)* ?/3/11.
8487 *(new)* 7/3/31.

SHEDS:
Trafford Park.
Langwith Junction ?/?/?.
Colwick 20/12/30.

RENUMBERED:
3919 3/4/25.

CONDEMNED: 13/10/36.
Cut up at Doncaster.

3920

Neilson 4407.

To traffic 12/1891.

REPAIRS:
Don. ?/?—?/8/11.**G**.
Don. 24/1—6/5/22.**G**.
Don. 4/3—11/7/25.**G**.
To Service Stock 22/11/28.
Don. 8/6—17/8/31.**G**.
Don. 9/8—9/9/33.**G**.
Rebuilt to J55.
Don. 23/3—25/4/36.**H**.
Don. 7—28/8/37.**L**.
Don. 22/4—13/5/39.**G**.
Don. 25/3—8/4/42.**L**.
Don. 16/1—13/2/43.**L**.
Don. 10—13/5/44.**L**.
Don. 4/1—3/2/45.**G**.
Don. 23/2—16/3/46.**L**.
Don. 21/12/46—4/1/47.**L**.
Don. 14—21/6/47.**L**.
Don. 28/6—3/7/48.**G**.
Don. 6—10/9/48.**L**.
Don. 22/2—2/3/49.**L**.
Don. 27/6—1/7/49.**C/L**.
Don. 1—5/9/49.**C/L**.

BOILERS:
920.
6996 *(new)* ?/8/11.
6996 reno. S.B.281 22/11/28.
8308 (exJ4 4084) reno. S.B.408 9/9/33.
7816 (exJ4 092) reno. S.B.761 3/2/45.

SHEDS:
Colwick.
Doncaster Works 22/11/28.

RENUMBERED:
3920 11/7/25.
4800 9/4/30.
4990 11/1/37.
8319 15/3/46.
68319 3/7/48.

WITHDRAWN: 22/11/28.
CONDEMNED: 23/6/50. *(per Accounts Register).*
Cut up at Doncaster .

No.3783 changed to the later parallel shank type buffers but kept the Westinghouse equipment from fitting on 26th February 1921 to 10th March 1934 withdrawal. Note that it also had carriage heating facility with connection also at the front end.

Until after the LNER took over, the original type of forward sanding remained with the delivery point some distance from the wheel, and some were not altered, amongst these being Nos.3153A, 3689, 3785 and 3790.

(above) **From 1925 the majority were fitted with longer sandpipes at the front, curved round the brake hanger, to place sand closer to the wheel.**

No.3851 presents a curious case of showing no evidence of piping connected with any type of injector. Those with faceplate type had an overflow pipe from the cab and then at a right angle to discharge by the side of the ashpan as shown on No.494N on the following page.

Apart from having no coal rails, No.3790 was unusual in keeping the original type of Stirling injector, whereas most changed to faceplate mounting.

In the summer of 1935, the Doncaster works shunter No.4800 was painted silver and grey with black letters and numbers, as trial painting for A4 class engines then being built. On 25th April 1936 it reverted to its unlined black.

Only two J55 carried L&NER, No.916 ex works 10th February 1923 still in GNR style and on grey paint. The other was No.918, ex works 16th June 1923 which was in black with red lining and 12in. numbers on the tank. On the next two, Nos.678 (30th June 1923) and 496 (18th August 1923), the ampersand was not included.

Seven then had the area suffix N added to their number, six in 1923 - 638A (6th September), 397 (7th September), 494 (27th October), 809 (8th November), 633A (16th November), 673 (15th December) - and one in 1924, No.912 (2nd February). No.494 had the Duplicate letter A added 29th December 1923.

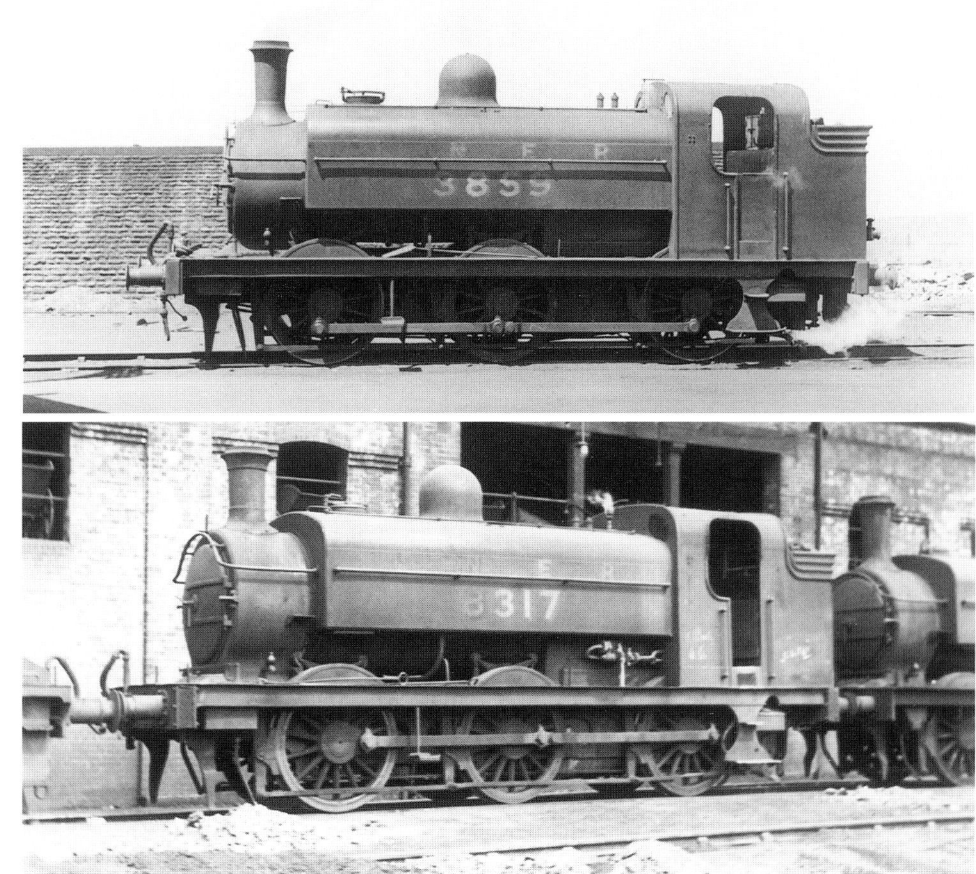

Starting with No.3851 on 16th February 1924, the full LNER number was used, and red lining was applied until the June 1928 economies took effect.

Only three were left to be affected by the wartime and post-war changes. No.3859 carried only NE from 9th January 1943 but on 12th January 1946 had LNER again. On Monday 17th June 1946 Doncaster shed renumbered it to 8317 in normal 12in. transfers which it kept to 24th December 1948 withdrawal.

The other one in Running Stock, No.3908 would have only NE from 18th March 1944 and did not have LNER restored. On Sunday 26th May 1946 Doncaster shed changed it to 8318 using small stencils. In blacking out the old number, they appear to have also obliterated the NE. It was withdrawn 27th May 1947 still in the style shown.

After losing the experimental silver-grey paint (*see* opposite, top), No.4800 regained normal livery which it kept when renumbered 4990 on 11th January 1937. From 3rd February 1945 it had only NE but LNER was restored 15th March 1946 when it was renumbered 8319 at a Light repair. From a General repair 3rd July 1948, it came out as No.68319 with the BRITISH RAILWAYS lettering on its tank sides. It remained in that style to its 23rd June 1950 withdrawal which made J55 class extinct.

From the driving wheels the rear spacing and the firebox casing were 8in. shorter than on J54 and the tanks were also 8in. shorter and 3in. narrower. At Grouping, Nos.608A, 612 and 615 had boilers of the original type but with faceplate injectors.

Ivatt decided against any replacement boilers being built for this class so the survivors had to make do with second-hand boilers adapted to suit them. In February 1908 No.611 got a boiler from an older saddletank just withdrawn. The barrel was 3in. shorter so the smokebox had to be extended and the firebox casing was 4in. shorter so it did not project into the cab by that amount as previously. Injectors were also the Stirling under-tank type. It became No.3611 on 29th August 1925. No.613 got a similar boiler in July 1910 and was lettered L&NER from 31st March 1923.

In 1924/5 the other three needed replacement boilers and the 4ft $2^{1}/_{2}$in. domed variety from withdrawn 0-4-4 tanks was adapted to serve them. They became LNER black with single red lining when ex works with their 4ft 2°in. boilers as follows: No.3615 on 21st June 1924, No.3608A on 16th August 1924 and No.3612 on 1st August 1925. Note that No.3615 had its front sandpipes lengthened and curved round the brake hanger. It also had a Stirling brass cover to its safety valves. These boilers had faceplate injectors.

CLASS J 56

3608A

Doncaster 217.

To traffic 2/1877.

REPAIRS:
Don. ?/?—?/8/95.**G**.
Don. 6/11/23—16/8/24.**G**.
Don. 25/11/27—3/2/28.**G**.

BOILERS:
608.
608 *(new)* ?/8/95.
1531 *(exGNR G3 762 4' 2½" domed)* 16/8/24.

SHEDS:
Lincoln.
New England *by* 23/8/27.
Boston 14/6/30.
New England 30/10/30.

RENUMBERED:
'**A**' *added* 4/19.
3608A 16/8/24.

CONDEMNED: 8/12/32.
Cut up at Doncaster.

3611

Doncaster 223.

To traffic 5/1877.

REPAIRS:
Don. ?/?—?/2/08.**G**.
Don. 1/5—7/7/23.**G**.
Don. 21/5—29/8/25.**G**.

BOILERS:
611.
6876 *(exGNR J12 162)* ?/2/08.

SHED:
Doncaster.

RENUMBERED:
3611 29/8/25.

CONDEMNED: 13/1/28.
Cut up at Doncaster.

3612

Doncaster 226.

To traffic 7/1877.

REPAIRS:
Don. ?/?—?/11/93.**G**.
Don. ?/?—?/9/11.**G**.
Don. 27/10/20—5/3/21.**G**.
Don. 8/12/24—1/8/25.**G**.

BOILERS:
612.
612 *(new)* ?/11/93.
613 *(ex613)* ?/9/11.
1533 *(exG2 694 4' 2½" domed)* 1/8/25.

SHED:
King's Cross.

RENUMBERED:
3612 1/8/25.

CONDEMNED: 10/10/28.
Cut up at Doncaster.

---

(3)613

Doncaster 228.

To traffic 9/1877.

REPAIRS:
Don. ?/?—?/7/96.**G**.
Don. ?/?—?/7/10.**G**.
Don. 15/11/22—31/3/23.**G**.

BOILERS:
613.
613 *(new)* ?/7/96.
7031 *(exGNR J12 166)* ?/7/10.

SHED:
Colwick.

RENUMBERED:
Believed not to have been renumbered.

CONDEMNED: 16/11/25.
Cut up at Doncaster.

3615

Doncaster 229.

To traffic 11/1877.

REPAIRS:
Don. ?/?—?/7/95.**G**.
Don. 7/11/23—21/6/24.**G**.

BOILERS:
615.
615 *(new)* ?/7/95.
7127 *(exGNR G1 826 4' 2½" domed)* 21/6/24.

SHED:
King's Cross.

RENUMBERED:
3615 21/6/24.

CONDEMNED: 9/2/27.
Cut up at Doncaster.

(below) **After 10th October 1928 No.3608A was the sole survivor and it kept its red lining to withdrawal on 8th December 1932 having last been ex works on 3rd February 1928. Its 1907 built boiler had an Ivatt cast iron enclosure to its safety valves, and it kept its original short sandpipes at the front.**

Two more engines, Nos.144 and 149, built at Doncaster in May and June 1892, completed the class. They had enclosed cabs and built-up bunkers, with short chimneys and safety valve covers but by Grouping No.144A had a standard cast 3ft 3in. chimney. Note the GNR load class 'F' and the LNER load class 3 collars on the vacuum brake standpipe.

The other 1892 engine, No.149A continued to be an oddity and remained below 11ft 6in. height from rail level through to its 5th August 1931 withdrawal. Ex works 8th January 1927, it had been fitted with this 4ft $2^{1}/_{2}$in. domed boiler from withdrawn Class J56 No.3615 for which the cab had to be extended 8in. forward to cope with the shorter firebox. With this 4ft $2^{1}/_{2}$in. boiler a short built-up chimney was carried and it was also the only one to have three coal rails. Note that its front sand pipes were lengthened.

CLASS J 57

3684

Doncaster 347.

To traffic 12/1882.

REPAIRS:
Don. ?/?—?/6/12.**G**.
Don. 14/12/21—25/2/22.**G**.
Don. 13/8—7/11/25.**G**.
Don. 5/3—12/5/28.**G**.

BOILERS:
684.
7120 *(new)* ?/6/12.

SHEDS:
King's Cross.
Hatfield 7/7/23.
King's Cross *after* 6/25.

RENUMBERED:
3684 7/11/25.

CONDEMNED: 26/9/30.
Cut up at Doncaster.

3685

Doncaster 348.

To traffic 12/1882.

REPAIRS:
Don. ?/?—?/8/11.**G**.
Don. ?/?—?/11/17.**G**.
Don. 5/6—7/8/20.**G**.
Don. 17/11/24—7/2/25.**G**.
Don. 15/9—16/11/27.**G**.
Don. 2—23/11/29.**G**.
Don. 13/8—17/9/32.**G**.
Don. 6—20/4/35.**G**.

BOILERS:
685.
855 *(ex J54 855)* ?/8/11.
7386 *(new: 4'-5"domed)* ?/11/17.
8313 *(new: 4'-5")* 23/11/29.

SHEDS:
King's Cross.
Hatfield 7/3/28.
King's Cross 1/9/29.
Doncaster 13/4/36.

RENUMBERED:
3685 7/2/25.

CONDEMNED: 17/6/38.
Cut up at Doncaster.

3686

Doncaster 364.

To traffic 3/1884.

REPAIRS:
Don. ?/?—?/6/11.**G**.
Don. 19/5—19/8/22.**G**.
Don. 12/3—21/6/24.**G**.
Don. 20/7/29. *Not Repaired.*

BOILERS:
686.
6998 *(new)* ?/6/11.

SHEDS:
King's Cross.
Ardsley *by* 29/6/27.

RENUMBERED:
3686 21/6/24.

CONDEMNED: 10/8/29.
Cut up at Doncaster.

3687

Doncaster 366.

To traffic 3/1884.

REPAIRS:
Don. ?/?—?/3/04.**G**.
Don. 22/10/20—26/2/21.**G**.
Don. 16/2—9/5/25.**G**.
Don. 17/8—1/10/26.**L**.
Don. 30/8—6/10/28.**G**.

BOILERS:
687.
1273 *(new)* ?/3/04.
8148 *(new 4'-5"domed)* 6/10/28.

SHED:
King's Cross.

RENUMBERED:
3687 9/5/25.

CONDEMNED: 11/11/30.
Cut up at Doncaster.

3134A

Doncaster 516.

To traffic 11/1890.

REPAIRS:
Don. 7/10—8/12/20.**G**.
Don. 19/12/23—14/6/24.**G**.
Don. 12/8—20/11/26.**G**.
Don. 14/8—18/9/29.**G**.

BOILERS:
134.
904 *(ex J54 904)* 8/12/20.
1454 *(4'-5"domed)* 14/6/24.
1533 *(ex J56 3612: 4'-2½")* 18/9/29.

SHED:
Grantham.

RENUMBERED:
134A 12/05.
3134A 14/6/24.

CONDEMNED: 24/3/32.
Cut up at Doncaster.

3140A

Doncaster 517.

To traffic 9/1890.

REPAIRS:
Don. ?/?—?/11/17.**G**.
Don. 6/2—27/5/22.**G**.
Don. 14/5—18/7/25.**G**.
Don. 8/3—10/4/26.**L**.
Don. 10—30/8/29.**G**.

BOILERS:
140.
7383 *(new 4'-5"domed)* ?/11/17.
6998 *(ex3686 4'-0°"domeless)* 30/8/29

SHED:
Doncaster.

RENUMBERED:
Duplicate '**A**' added 6/06.
3140A 18/7/25.

CONDEMNED: 3/10/32.
Cut up at Doncaster.

3144A

Doncaster 577.

To traffic 5/1892.

REPAIRS:
Don. ?/?—?/11/11.**G**.
Don. ?/?—?/6/19.**G**.
Don. 5/1—3/6/22.**G**.
Don. 13/8—18/10/24.**G**.
Don. 29/5—29/6/29.**G**.

BOILERS:
144.
914 *(exJ54 914)* ?/11/11.
636 *(exJ54 636A)* ?/6/19.
6905 *(exJ54 855)* 3/6/22.

SHEDS:
King's Cross.
Hornsey *by* 6/5/24.

RENUMBERED:
Duplicate '**A**' added 8/06.
3144A 18/10/24.

CONDEMNED: 7/10/33.
Cut up at Doncaster.

3149A

Doncaster 580.

To traffic 6/1892.

REPAIRS:
Don. ?/?—?/6/10.**G**.
Don. 21/3—11/6/21.**G**.
Don. 28/2—5/7/24.**G**.
Don. 14/9/26—8/1/27.**G**.
Don. 21/3—13/4/29.**G**.

BOILERS:
149.
859 *(exJ54 859)* ?/6/10.
7127 *(exJ56 3615 4'-2½"domed)* 8/1/27.

SHEDS:
Hitchin.
King's Cross 22/12/23.

RENUMBERED:
Duplicate '**A**' added 9/06.
3149A 5/7/24.

CONDEMNED: 5/8/31.
Cut up at Doncaster.

In November 1917 Nos.140A and 685 were rebuilt with Ivatt 4ft 5in. diameter domed boilers in place of the original 4ft $0^1/_2$in. domeless type, but no separate classification was given as was the case with J54 to J55 class. No.3685 remained thus to withdrawal 17th June 1938, when it was the last of class, but No.3140A reverted to its original state 30th August 1929. In the meantime the LNER rebuilt two more with 4ft 5in. boilers, Nos.3134A (14th June 1924) and 3687 (6th October 1928). The latter kept its 4ft 5in. boiler to its 11th November 1930 withdrawal, but No.3134A received a 4ft $2^1/_2$in. domed boiler off withdrawn J56 No.3612 on 14th September 1929. No.3149A also received a 4ft $2^1/_2$in. boiler (off J56 No.3615) 8th January 1927 to withdrawal on 5th August 1931 (*see* previous illustration).

Ex works 30th August 1929 No.3140A had reverted to a domeless 4ft $0^1/_2$in. diameter, 10ft 1in. long boiler from No.3686 which had just been withdrawn, but No.3140A kept its higher cab into which circular windows could now replace the previous oval ones. With the cab positioned 1in. to the rear, the splasher casing to the rear wheels could just be discerned.

The two with enclosed cabs were the only ones to keep the cut-down versions of the brass safety valve cover, and No.3144A got footsteps on its bunker, but only on the right hand side.

At Grouping all were in GNR unlined grey paint. Note that in this 7th May 1921 photograph No.686 had still not been fitted with coal rails, and it had parallel shank front buffers with end collars and solid spindles.

(below) **After the LNER came into being the first to get black paint with single red lining was No.3134A, ex works 14th June 1924, so all eight went straight to LNER livery and 1924 numbers. The four on the Duplicate List carried 'A' from the following dates: 134A (December 1905), 140A (June 1906), 144A (August 1906), 149A (September 1906).**

Only Nos.3684 and 3686 retained red lining to withdrawal. No.3687, ex works 6th October 1928 was the first in plain black and No.3685, out on 23rd November 1929 completed this change. Because No.3685 was the only one to have a works visit after 1929, it was alone in having plating put behind its coal rails when ex works 17th September 1932.

Only Nos.3687 (6th October 1928) and 3685 (23rd November 1929) changed to new 4ft 5in. diameter boilers having Ross 'pop' safety valves. No.3685 was the only one noted with its whistle above the cab roof. With their higher pitch and standard length built-up chimney, the height from rail level was 12ft 7in. At its 17th September 1932 repair, No.3685 got a modern injector but kept the taper shank buffers.

Although from 7th October 1933 No.3685 was the sole survivor, it had another General repair and when ex works 20th April 1935, three changes of detail had been made; buffers had become parallel shank type, front sand pipes had been restored to pre-1925 style and the cab roof had acquired a storm sheet. Withdrawal of No.3685 on 17th June 1938 made Class J57 extinct.